Ignite YOUR Power Within

Ignite YOUR POWER WITHIN

14 SIMPLE, PROVEN METHODS TO RECLAIM YOUR HAPPINESS AND JOY

CHRISSY BARIBAULT-ORTIZ & RAEANN BARIBAULT SCHWARTZ

NEW YORK

LONDON • NASHVILLE • MELBOURNE • VANCOUVER

Ignite YOUR Power Within

14 Simple, Proven Methods to Reclaim Your Happiness and Joy

Published in New York, New York, by Morgan James Publishing. Morgan James is a trademark of Morgan James, LLC. www.MorganJamesPublishing.com

Proudly distributed by Publishers Group West®

ISBN 9781636986036 paperback
ISBN 9781636986043 ebook
Library of Congress Control Number:
2024948766

Cover Design by:
Ale Urquide

Interior Design by:
Chris Treccani
www.3dogcreative.net

Morgan James is a proud partner of Habitat for Humanity Peninsula and Greater Williamsburg. Partners in building since 2006.

Get involved today! Visit: www.morgan-james-publishing.com/giving-back

For the readers brave enough to pick up a book like this, and trust in your Power to B. Your commitment to B your best self makes this world a more beautiful place. Take good care of you and keep leading with your heart.

xxoo
Love,
Chrissy and Raeann

CONTENTS

ACKNOWLEDGMENTS

Thank you to the Power to B community members, our customers and friends, who took the time to share their stories for the book. Your stories will help someone who reads this book, and your vulnerability has the power to change lives. We love you for your kindness. You are why we do what we do.

Thank you to Ms. Rachel Hollis for writing the first book that ever stopped us in our tracks and changed the trajectory of our lives.

Thank you to the instructors and coaches in the Peloton community for providing us with a daily dose of happy. You probably don't know you're our inspiration but you uplift us every single day, mentally and physically.

Thank you to Maria Chapman and the Connected Ghostwriting team for organizing, interviewing, and making our ideas shine. We appreciate you for your creative energy, for your gifts, and for allowing us the ability to share our story. You made this happen.

Thank you to the team at Morgan James Publishing for your guidance and vision in getting this book into HER hands.

Thank you to Christine Lee for believing in The Power to B, for the Bada** Women of the Week program, and for writing the foreword.

Thank you to Nuriye Rumeli, Dr. Michael Stokes, Georgia Homsany, and Jennifer Moore for your contribution to the book. Your expertise enriches these pages and will help us have an even greater impact.

Thank you to our Baribault Jewelers family for believing in the vision, and for showing up with an open heart every single day.

Stephen Alexander, thank you for awakening our eyes to the power of the B.

Thank you to our family for *ALWAYS* being there. Mom, Dad, Danny, Evan, Lewis and Nichole, and most of all Scarlet, Kash, Eva, Zane, Raven, Lewy, Lila and Cody.

- Thank you, Mom, for your incredible strength and ability to tenaciously support our family.
- Thank you, Dad, for always radiating positivity, even at 5:00 a.m.
- Thank you Danny—for being my biggest cheerleader, my sounding board, and my partner in everything. You're my rock with unwavering love and support and for that, I am forever grateful to have you as my partner in this journey. All my Love, Chrissy
- Thank you Evan for your partnership, loyalty & love. I am forever grateful for your willingness to always prioritize me, Eva, Zane & Raven and for your encouragement on this journey of growth together. Love. Rae
- Thank you, Grandma Dolly for showing us how to live with purpose & for being our guiding light, XXOO.

We love you all beyond words.

Thank you to the Universe, and for all the signs that this book was the next right thing.

To Rae, Thank you for being present in the journey, for all the times you helped make me feel seen in all the ways you do when I sometimes couldn't. I'll B forever grateful. Cheers to you sis. Xxoo, Chrissy

To Chrissy, you are my born sister but my chosen best friend, life supporter, partner in all things, and always know how to raise me up, give me new perspective, and grow together. Life is better with you. Love, Rae

FOREWORD

It was during the buzz of the Academy Awards season a few years back when I first encountered the inspiring story of Chrissy and Rae, two remarkable women from Glastonbury whose elegant bracelets were making waves among celebrities.

As a morning show host on 96.5 TIC, I'm always on the lookout for compelling stories that resonate with our audience. Their story, tied neatly with the glamor of Hollywood, caught my attention, but I soon discovered there was much more to these women than their moment in the limelight.

Chrissy and Rae, both beautiful, funny, articulate, and successful moms, had faced significant personal challenges. They struggled with fertility issues, an ordeal that eventually inspired the creation of The Power to B line. The pieces they designed were not just jewelry; they were personal affirmations, a source of strength during their toughest times.

This resonated deeply with me, reminding me of something my late, beloved grandfather, a U.S. Air Force Colonel who was a veteran of WWII and Vietnam, often emphasized: the importance of a Positive Mental Attitude (PMA). He mentioned that, before climbing in the cockpit, pilots had a checklist and PMA was at the top. He believed that without the right mindset, one shouldn't even think of taking on the day's challenges—a philosophy that Chrissy and Rae embodied.

When I was asked to write this foreword, it was a no-brainer. Having featured countless "bada** women" who conquered both monumental and everyday battles in the "Bada** Woman of the Week" series in partnership with The Power to B brand, it felt right to celebrate Chrissy and Rae's milestone. They had turned their trials into a source of empowerment for many others.

My personal encounter with their Powerwords came during my first interview with them, a moment that unexpectedly moved me. Asked to choose my Powerword, I selected "Bbada**"—a word that gained profound personal significance as I ran marathons, went skydiving, raised two sons, and then succeeded in my first battle with cancer. Now, as I face cancer once more, my "Bbada**" necklace and bracelet serve as daily reminders of my strength and resilience. "How would a bada** handle this?" I often ask myself. This mantra has not only helped me but has also woven itself into the culture of our morning show, enriching relationships around the station, and inspiring both listeners and colleagues alike.

I had the pleasure of interviewing Erica Farber, Former President & CEO at Radio Advertising Bureau. During the interview she noted how men often pursue opportunities even when minimally qualified, whereas women may hold back despite being more than capable. In radio—a male dominated industry—it is frustrating to see women struggle to achieve the same level of recognition, pay equality, and opportunity for promotion that men often take for granted. Chrissy and Rae are countering this trend, urging women to focus on their strengths and embrace their full potential. This book, Ignite your POWER Within, is a testament to their journey and a toolkit for anyone ready to rediscover their joy, purpose, and inherent power.

As part of the Bad** Woman of the Week, I've had the privilege of interviewing many incredible women and many of their stories are included at the end of this book. I hope you see yourself in these stories. I hope you let their resilience strengthen you.

What each of these women have is a connection to their Power to B—and that's what I want for you. It's the reason I was so excited to write this foreword. Women need to remember that they can harness their inner power to accomplish anything from toilet training a toddler to starting the next Fortune 500 company.

I have a poster that I saw while running the Hartford marathon. It says "I have met my hero and SHE is within me." I always think of that poster and how it really resonates with me and calls forth my inner strength. I feel the same way about Bbada**. It's within me! It's within ALL OF US! We are our own heroes and bada**es.

So, get out there, focus on your strengths, cultivate your power, and, most importantly, Byou.

Welcome to your transformation.

> **—Christine Lee,** radio host and co-founder
> of Rise and Shine CT

INTRODUCTION

From Chrissy

When I was a child, just learning to spell properly, I used to sit in the back of my parents' beige station wagon and imagine that if I could create the perfect unique magic word like a magic spell, wondrous things would happen outside my window. If I wrote a series of these most unique never written or spoken perfect combination of letters, perhaps a rainbow might instantly appear in the sky. Another string of symbols might conjure up a unicorn to gallop along that rainbow. I believed words could B magic, even at that young age, and I still believe it today.

In fact, I believe so strongly in the magical power of words, My sister Rae and I created an entire jewelry line of Powerwords because creating jewelry is what we do. Don't worry, I'm not here to sell you jewelry. I'm here to share our power word practice with you because I want you to believe in magic again.

Hey there, I'm Chrissy. I am a mother of two miracle babies (as if they all aren't miracles), but that's what I like to call mine), a jewelry designer, a certified health coach, a wife of a police officer, a daughter, and a sister, but none of those roles really describe who I am. I am so much more and, at the same time, so much less than those roles. I am loving, passionate, and determined. I am creative, adventurous, and am also an overthinker who wrestles with self-doubt at times. I am spiritual, energetic, and grateful. Sometimes I feel anxious and overwhelmed. I am silly (when I remember to be playful) and I know when to get down to business. I hate doing the dishes, and I Love connecting with people.

Mostly, though, I am a firm believer in the power inside of you and me and signs and that all things happen for us exactly as and when they are supposed to. I'm so glad you picked up this book. I want this book to feel like a conversation—one that is fun, playful, also serious. I want to offer you the perfect amount of information and inspiration. I want to offer a helpful and powerful chat on how a Powerword practice helped me make it through the hard things while still enjoying the journey (at least most of the time).

From Rae

Hi, I'm Raeann, but I often go by Rae. Chrissy and I wrote different introductions for a couple of reasons. Mostly, though, it's because we know that some of you will connect more with Chrissy's story and some of you will connect more with mine. I often find writing biographies of myself difficult because, as with most of you, I am constantly changing and feel like I meet a new version of myself every five years or so as I move through different stages of life. The version of me that exists now as you read these words may be different in some ways than the version of me who wrote this book. So, the best I can do is tell you who I am today.

I am a mom of three small children, an entrepreneur, a free thinker, a wife, jewelry designer & marketing specialist, but that isn't who I am. When I ask women to tell me about themselves, I get a list of their roles in society, not all that different from how I began introducing myself here. I'm much more intrigued when someone tells me about who they really are instead of about their roles. I love when people are in tune with themselves and their character. I like knowing who you are based on what you believe and what you enjoy doing because that helps paint a picture of your soul. Since that's what I find most interesting I'll offer you the same.

I am a believer in karma and a positive mindset. I am spiritual not religious. I have a touch of OCD, and am a Taurus through and through (to my detriment sometimes). I value family above everything else, which is why I make sure I take care of myself. I cannot serve my family well unless I am fulfilled. I love to cook, I love learning about food and where it comes from. I am passionate about grounding, planting and growing what my climate allows me to. I love learning about people's families and their stories. I find sibling dynamics incredibly interesting. I find peace near the water. I love prosecco, because I think anything with bubbles is more fun. I also love all things sparkly—diamonds, Pellegrino, champagne, the sun hitting the water, and the innocent twinkle in my children's eyes.

I believe in energy, and reiki, the power of the universe, and manifesting the life you want.

I am a woman committed to getting to know myself as I grow through life. My purpose in life is to challenge societal norms that are put on women and prove to myself and others that you can have it all, do whatever you want, and no one sets limits on you except yourself. You can do whatever you want and need to fuel you—mind, body, and soul—if you decide it's important in your life. I am a non-traditionalist when it comes to gender roles in our homes, in business, and in society.

I knew, watching women of previous generations, that I didn't want the traditional household arrangement and life, that I would never choose one thing—that I could have a rich, multifaceted life. I want to show other women they can flourish and live the life they want. My life doesn't look the way society says it should…but the second you decide to reject those barriers you get to actually live your life.

What is the life you've wanted to create? Why haven't you allowed yourself the joy of experiencing the things you want? Who told you you don't get to be, do, and have it all? The Power to B represents a lifestyle and a mindset that you have the power to create the life you want right now, today, inside your soul. You don't need permission, you don't need a life coach, and you don't need any fancy solutions. All you need is to remember the essence of who you are and what you want. You need to remember how to dream, and then you need to take responsibility and claim your dreams.

When was the last time you set a goal? Was it lofty, unrestrained, and true? Or, did you hold back and set a goal that was realistic and socially acceptable? I want the Powerwords in these chapters to help you remember how to dream, how to embrace your true self, and how to live your life with the energy and direction you always wanted.

I'm so glad you're here, and I can't wait to see what Powerwords you use in your life.

CHAPTER 1:

The Power to B

Let's Get Real

There was a time decades ago when women were taught that the best they could hope for was life as a wife and mother. Once you achieved motherhood, you'd be fulfilled and want for nothing more. It was a prideful role to manage a household and raise a family, but that's no longer the case. In the world we live in today, expectations have risen for women.

The overstimulation that is now normal blows our mind—women have to have a career, we have to contribute because things are more expensive, we have to have a happy, healthy marriage, feel joy every day so you don't seem like a bitch, run a household, make meals, handle home upkeep, and be a mom. This level of stimulation isn't normal, but it's expected.

We must make it through college with high marks, get married, but not too early, and definitely not too late. We should have children unless we don't want them, but we shouldn't have too many children. If we have fertility trouble or miscarriages, we should suffer in silence. Our homes must be beautifully decorated but not too stuffy. We must be neat and organized, but we mustn't nag others to meet our expectations for upkeep. We should use gentle parenting techniques and ensure our toddlers never inconvenience the world with a tantrum on a plane or in a grocery store. We have to be sexy enough to keep our husbands interested, but not too sexy that we are a threat to other women. Also, on that note, we are all a sisterhood and have to support one another, but not too much—we wouldn't want that other woman to get what we want. We should love our bodies, but we can't be conceited. We must age gracefully but not use anti-aging technology, unless we want to. Then, we should be upfront about it so others don't think we are naturally wrinkle-free, dark-haired goddesses.

Are you tired just reading that? You should be. We certainly are. There are many days when the pressure feels like it could eat us alive. On top of all these expectations that are placed on us as women—careers, being moms, marriage, relationships, kids, social media, health challenges, body image, etc.—we have to find time for what makes us happy. How?!?

We have to tap into our own power, cultivate inner strength, and figure out what noise we want to listen to and what we want to block out. It's time to be your own best cheerleader. It's up to you and the power you have inside you to ignite the changes into a more positive mindset, a more powerful way to self-talk, and find the gratitude within because we have no doubt in our minds, you are the driving force in your home.

This realization—that we are the driving forces in our homes—led us to create The Power to B brand.

The Power to B Is Born

Chrissy's Story

The practice came first: the very first time I remember needing a constant reminder was during a bad breakup. I put "one day at a time" on my phone lock screen. During that time, my sister saw me and gave me a necklace (a letter C in white gold and diamonds) and said, "This is your power Chrissy necklace. Wear it and remember the most powerful version of yourself." Then, every time a challenge came up, having that reminder worked. It gave me strength.

I started wondering how else I could use those reminders. I started using whiteboards and post it notes around the house to write reminders for myself. I got a tattoo of the word "faith" to remind myself that I could surrender. Then, after my marriage, I went through fertility treatments and kept using those written reminders and wearing my C necklace. When Rae entered a fertility struggle as well, we decided to move the practice to a bracelet because we'd see them all day, every day. We asked customers what words they'd most like to see, and then we started selling in our jewelry store and online. Customers asked for more and different power words and shared stories of how the power words helped them.

Rae's Story

After Chrissy's three years of fertility struggle, I began a similar struggle that also lasted three years. It was the most challenging time in my life. I felt challenged beyond my control. I never doubted that I was going to be a mom one day, but I knew internally that my goal was out of my hands, and I was not used to that. I was used to being able to set a goal and work to achieve it. Since this wasn't in my control, I had options. I could choose to experience the journey with a bit more grace instead of struggle, or it could lead me into an emotional spiral and a dark place. I know it does for so many women.

When we go through this as women, we question ourselves, our worth—why me? You feel guilty because your partner wants kids too. Why can't I give us what I'm supposed to give us as a woman? Why isn't my body working like it should? I had moments of feeling deep sadness and lots of self-doubt. My days started to feel darker. I'm not a dark spirit, but I definitely felt dark. We went to the Rise conference with Rachel Hollis. I had a pivotal moment where I realized I had a choice in how I felt going through this journey. I could empower myself and embrace the challenge, or I could not. I started to use power words and affirmations in the form of Post-its on my bathroom mirror every day to decide how I wanted to live in this journey. I needed to power up and be my own cheerleader.

I hadn't felt joy or gratitude in a while, so, I started writing, "Today I choose gratitude, today I choose joy." Every time I headed to a fertility appointment where the unexpected always happens, I chose to use those words to empower myself so I could be more accepting of what was to come. I didn't know what was on the other side, but I'm grateful. On my way to an appointment, hands clenching the steering wheel, white knuckles, I thought, "I really wish that post it from my mirror was on my windshield. Or, better yet, on my wrist to see every moment I needed it. Then I thought of the bracelets. When I needed the reminder most, they weren't there. I had Post-its on a paper calendar planner that said "breathe," and during the day I remember tapping it when I needed a moment. I started to see these little things having a huge impact. My state of mind shifted. I was suddenly aware of my emotions and the power of visual reminders in my life.

The Practice: Power to B—The Mind, Body, and Spirit-Care Practice to B a More Powerful You

This is the practice that helps us harness our inner power and move through life with more joy.

Pray and Pause: Pray for Clarity and Guidance

Chrissy

I had a panic attack right before starting this book, which I'll talk about more later. Sitting in the hospital, feeling the weight of the world, I said a prayer for clarity and guidance. It's funny how answers often find us when we simply pray and ask for them and how and when we least expect them yet need them most.

For me, it came during a heart-to-heart the next morning with Raeann. I woke up with her sitting next to my bed ready to share some thoughtful, powerful, and sisterly-like advice that I needed to hear, which was a catalyst for the next step I would take and, all of a sudden, things were a little bit clearer. Prayer answered (thanks, Rae!).

Rae

I don't pray in a traditional way; I am more faithful and spiritual than religious, so I don't pray for guidance, but I do give things space and time. Within days of surrendering and letting things go, clarity and guidance come to me. I used to plan, and then plan for the plan, then plan a backup plan. Once I had three kids, I had to prepare to throw those plans out the window because so much of life is unplannable. Being in the space of "I don't know what to do, but I know it will come to me" has been transformative.

Ownership: Decide How You Want to Feel Instead of How Things Make You Feel

Feeling overwhelmed, lost, or confused? We've been there. What we learned to do in these situations that took off so much pressure during an already confusing season of life is to give ourselves permission to simply focus on what feelings we want to feel more of. Then, we pick one and start there, in that moment, for the rest of that day, and then repeat tomorrow. For example, if we want to feel less stressed and more relaxed, we can go to our list of things that make us feel relaxed and promise ourselves to do one thing on this list today and then again tomorrow. Repeat.

Then, actually do what you promised because the promises we make to ourselves are most important to keep. By the time the week is through, you've started momentum and most likely will feel well on your way to more relaxed.

To start this practice, ask yourself, "SELF, what feelings do you want to create more of in your life?"

Chrissy

I wanted to feel lighter, happier, more playful, and relaxed in my day-to-day. I wanted to be more clear on my purpose, and I knew to do that, I first needed to cultivate more of the positive types of feelings I was lacking consistently. I knew if I could just focus on what it took to help me feel more relaxed and happier, I would already be well on my way to feeling less stressed, mentally and physically drained, and less overwhelmed. Maybe you too want to feel more excited and inspired and in a smoother rhythm each day. It all starts with awareness of what you want, calling the shots, making the promises to do, and then doing the things that work for you.

Rae

I wanted to seize complete control of my own experience of this one life I get to live. Do you want to be dependent on others, or do you want to be your own cheerleader? Many women feel dependent on the energy of their spouse, their families, and their coworkers—just because your others aren't on the same wavelength as you doesn't mean they have to affect your energy. Just because someone is in your space and in your life and having a hard time, a bad day, etc., that doesn't affect you and how you live your life. It's no one else's fault if you're unhappy every day. Taking ownership of that is not overwhelming; rather, it's freeing.

Wellness Matters: Have You Been Sleeping Well? Eating Well? Moving Well?

Never underestimate the power of a good wholesome snack or a solid nap, a hydrating glass of water, or a walk around the block. It's the small acts of self-care that often bring us back to our center. When was the last time you checked in with your body and gave it what it really needed?

Getting in tune with your body will help you determine what you need when you're feeling off. For both of us, a daily dose of endorphins has proved vital to our health.

Rae

During COVID-19, I was home with a three-year-old, an eighteen-month-old, and a newborn. I didn't have child care assistance, and I didn't have the time for exercise or self-care. At that time, I made the decision to make a change and create the energy I needed for the day. I now get up before the kids to get the endorphin rush in. I get up at 5:15 to work out, shower, journal, and make coffee before the kids get up. I realized I was never going to have the time so it was up to me to make the time for self-care because that is what makes me feel like the best me. I made other changes too. I don't drink alcohol regularly (though a social glass of prosecco is still a treat). I take the time to meal prep, eat healthy, exercise, hydrate, stretch, drink tea, and meditate on occasion because that is what makes me feel like my favorite version of me.

Do you catch yourself saying: "I wish I had time for myself, I wish I could?" Make the time. Time for yourself will never magically appear. Make it happen. You will never have "enough." You have to make your schedule reflect your priorities. Think of the phrase "favorite version of yourself" instead of "best version of yourself." What version of you do you like most? Now, go Bher.

Experience: What's Worked Before May Help You Now

Chrissy

There's power in your own history, and we often don't need to reinvent the wheel with things in life. Take a walk down memory lane and remember what brought you joy, what lifted your spirits, what made you feel beautiful and confident as hell. Keep a list—mine includes everything from reiki sessions to hot yoga, and even just making my nightly cup of tea. Let these past joys be your guide when the path gets foggy.

Rae

This is where journaling comes in for me. My daily journal is very simple. I take 5 minutes every day to journal because it helps me stay positive and grateful instead of shifting into that negative, overwhelmed space. Sometimes I have a hard day and need to flip through past pages of my journal to remind myself of the gratitude, successes, etc. Our brains remember more of the bad than the good. The more we stay consistent and remind ourselves what's worked before, the stronger we will be in the face of adversity.

RemindHer: Focus on Accomplishment and Gratitude

All you list-makers, this is your time to shine! Keeping a list of your triumphs, no matter how small, is like building a lighthouse in your own heart, one that shines through the darkest nights. When you question yourself, doubt your strength, or worry that you're going to mess it all up, this list will remind you of who you are, what you are capable of, and who you're working to become. We'll share more about how to do this in the coming chapters, but for now, find a small notebook you can carry with you and get ready to celebrate you.

We also encourage you to start a gratitude practice aligned with this practice of reminding yourself of all that you've done. You can use a journal for this, or just speak your gratitude out loud before you cozy up in bed every night. When you're in that stuck place or feeling off in some way, come back to your accomplishments and gratitude to recenter your spirit so you can continue building your dream life.

Rae

I start my journal every day with "What are you grateful for?" Some days that is easy, and other days writing my gratitude list is more challenging. But the more you focus on gratitude, the easier it becomes to make that list. Sometimes it's the cup of coffee I'm drinking at this moment. Some days it's I am grateful for health, kids, career—it can be anything big or small. They hold the same power. Writing down what you're grateful for every day will reset your mind to a more positive space. This practice although simple, is taken seriously and I have found a way to hold myself accountable to make sure I do it every day. You can hold yourself accountable in all sorts of ways. For me, I will not sip the coffee my husband lovingly makes me every morning until I've done my journal. The first comforting sip is my reward for staying consistent. Being positive is something we have to practice. The more we practice, the easier it becomes.

Test a New Way of Doing Things

Chrissy

Ever wanted to try something completely new or even just a bit out of your comfort zone? Now's the time. Whether it's a yoga retreat in Morocco, a tarot reading, or just trying coconut water for the first time—let curiosity lead the way to joy. Remember, life's too short to take too seriously.

Testing new things is how you get to know yourself. If you're not in tune with who you are and what makes you feel good, you aren't alone. There isn't a lot of time for tuning into ourselves in today's world. If you're in the habit of abandoning yourself so much you don't know who you are, how you want to live, and what your goals are, trying new things will help you figure it out.

| Rae |

We change so dramatically every five or so years, so you have to figure out how to meet yourself again. Female flamingos lose their vibrant pink color because they give their nutrients to their babies. They consume so little of the shrimp that turns them pink that by the time their babies are nearly grown, the mamas have nearly white feathers. As the mother of three littles, I know humans are no different. When I was a new mom, I was going through the motions of work, husband, kids, and marriage. But, I also know that you and I are in control of how and when we get our pink back. What brings your pink back?

Open Your Mind to Possibilities

When you catch yourself thinking, "What if it doesn't work? What if it all goes wrong?" We want you to stop yourself. Those thoughts come from fear, and fear will hold you back from the life you're meant to live. We'll guide you through how to do this in the chapters that follow, but for now, just practice turning those negative what-ifs into "What if it all exceeds my expectations?" Feel how your heart and mind open instantly with that shift in phrasing. Embrace the limitless possibility of who you could be, what you might do, and how you might feel.

B True to Who You Are

What are your values? Think about future you in every chapter. You know yourself better than anyone else knows you. No one knows who you were, who you are now, and who the future you is, but you do. You know where you came from, the struggles you've overcome, and the success you've enjoyed. You know where you are now, what lights you up, and what brings you down. And even if you don't know exactly who that future version of you is, she does. And she is rooting for you, praying for you, looking forward to meeting you someday soon. And it's safe to say if you haven't yet put much thought into future you, now is the perfect time.

What does she look like? How does she act? What's her day-to-day like? Starting to cultivate the future you and always keeping her in mind with your choices and actions is one of the most powerful pieces of advice I believe I can share. The you who already has what you want, living the life you can so easily dream of. Now it's time to be honest with yourself, time to meet her halfway. Anyone can have a dream and a plan, but most miss out on the action step piece. If you can take one action step every day for 365 days towards transforming into your future self your life will change significantly, and so will the way you *feel* in your life.

P ray and Pause: Pray for Clarity and Guidance

O wnership: Decide How You Want to Feel Instead

W ellness Matters: Are You Sleeping Well? Eating Well? Moving Well?

E xperience: What's Worked Before May Help You Now

R emindHER: Focus on Accomplishment and Gratitude

T est a New Way of Doing Things

O pen Your Mind to Possibilities

B True to Who You Are

Visual Reminders: Why They Matter

Visual reminders are more than just notes or objects that you might randomly come across; they are powerful tools that tap into your visual memory, acting as continuous cues to keep focused on your goals, aspirations, and the mindset you strive to uphold. Here's why they work for us and how they can significantly influence anyone's journey toward creating the life they want.

Constant Reinforcement: Seeing something repeatedly can reinforce a message or behavior in our minds. By strategically placing visual reminders where we frequently look—like on our mirrors, the lock screen of our phones, next to our coffee pots, or on our wrists—we create an environment that continuously nudges us towards our desired mindset or goal.

Immediate Motivation: These reminders act as instant motivators. On days when we feel disconnected from our goals or overwhelmed by challenges, a quick glance at a meaningful symbol, word, or phrase can reignite our motivation and remind us of what we're working towards.

Cue for Action: They serve as cues for action, transforming abstract intentions into tangible steps. For example, our bracelets engraved with "Bfearless" not only remind us of our capacity to overcome fears but also prompt us to take actions that reflect courage and confidence.

Anchor to Positive Emotions: Visual reminders can also anchor us to the positive emotions associated with our goals. Each time we see a post it note that says "I feel grateful," it can trigger a moment of reflection on the things we appreciate, enhancing our overall sense of well-being.

Clarity in Complexity: In our complex daily lives, it's easy to get lost in the noise. Visual reminders help maintain clarity by keeping our focus on what truly matters. They act as beacons guiding us through our day-to-day decisions and interactions, ensuring that we stay aligned with our deeper values and long-term objectives.

Customization and Personal Connection: The beauty of visual reminders lies in their ability to be deeply personalized. Whether it's a custom-designed bracelet, a specially chosen wallpaper for our phones, or a handwritten note on our mirrors, these reminders are uniquely ours. This personal connection not only enhances their significance but also increases their effectiveness.

By integrating visual reminders into our environment, we're essentially setting up a landscape that continuously communicates with us, encouraging, guiding, and sometimes even challenging us to grow and stay aligned with our journey toward joy and fulfillment. They remind us that every day, we have the power to take actions that bring us closer to the life we envision.

You can place visual reminders everywhere!

- Lock the screen on your phone.
- Bedroom or bathroom mirror Post-it note.
- Coffee pot.
- On your laptop.
- Bracelet (our favorite, obviously).
- Calendar.
- Refrigerator.

Embrace Your Power to B

Our first Powerword for the Power to B collection was Bstrong. At that time, we needed strength to continue on our journey to become mothers. We started talking to women that came into the jewelry store and asking what their power words were—what words would empower them every day. When women started wearing these bracelets, the five most popular ere Bstrong, Bfearless, Blimitless, and Bbad***. We heard stories of how these bracelets were helping women through health challenges, relationship challenges, and career challenges. We put them on bracelets because they're easy to see all day, every day. We have necklaces too, but the bracelets are more powerful because you can see them all day.

The jewelry is just a tangible item, but The Power to B is not about jewelry. You have the power to get wherever you want to be and have the energy and emotional state you want. The power is within you. You can't expect to have cheerleaders in your life all the time, so you have to be your own cheerleader. Choosing to empower yourself with self-talk, affirmations, and power words, and living your life by leading yourself in that way will create a better life. Whether you choose to use these techniques, leading with gratitude and inspiring yourself and being the best version of yourself is what The Power to B is all about.

> RemindHer: The Power to B is about recognizing the strength within you and cultivating that power daily to navigate life's challenges and joys.

CHAPTER 2:

RemindHer

———— ▬ ————

Have you been feeling lost lately?

Stress, overwhelm, depression, anxiety, despair, grief, dread, discouragement, exhaustion, confusion? No matter where we are and what we're struggling with, here's the good news… Struggle and challenge, though uncomfortable, are completely natural. We want you to use this book as a RemindHer (our version of a reminder . . . we'll explain it more later) that it's okay not to be okay while navigating through hard times. Negative feelings are natural and can be challenging for all of us.

Let's start with something quick and easy. We can start today to give these hard feelings a bit less power and see if a simple tweak can make us feel a bit better. Try this… let's say we're wrestling with anxiety. Instead of saying "I am anxious," we can change the words to "I feel anxious" to remind ourselves that this hard feeling, even though tough, won't last forever and is not a permanent part of us. We can swap anxious for stressed, overwhelmed, confused, sad, etc.

17

Now here is a key element we will talk about throughout the book: create a "RemindHer." Our human brains are wired to forget half of what we learn and do, so conquering challenges or creating new habits one by one can be accomplished by setting a visual reminder where we can see it. Seeing the reminder repeatedly helps our brains create new pathways so we don't get lost in the hamster wheel of negative thoughts so easily. It can be as simple, though not always easy, as that. For this example, we might recommend writing "I feel" on a post it note and sticking it near our mirrors, in our cars, at our desks, and anywhere else we feel that feeling creeping in.

It's simple, and it works. It's how our brains are wired up. Research shows that to learn new things, our brains need to develop new knowledge structures called "schemas." So, our brains only learn what is a priority and discard the loads of other information we see and hear every day. RemindHers help build those new knowledge structures.

Practices like posting RemindHers help build these mental structures and memories by ensuring we remember important information. Here's how this works:

- **Repetition Helps Memory:** When we post RemindHer, we see the information over and over again. This repetition helps our brains remember it better, making it stick in our memory.

- **Triggering Memory:** RemindHers act like little hints that help us remember important things. These hints can remind us of what we need to do.

- **Fitting Into What We Know:** Seeing RemindHers regularly helps us fit this new information into what we already know. For example, if we see a RemindHer to "drink water" every day, we'll eventually start to remember to stay hydrated without needing the reminder.

- **Making Things Easier:** RemindHers help by taking some of the pressure off our brains. Instead of trying to remember everything on our own, we can use RemindHers to help us focus on more important tasks.
- **Learning New Things:** For new or hard tasks, Remind-Hers can help us learn and remember. If we're learning something new, posting those RemindHers around our room helps us remember them better and makes learning easier.

Now, let's try this together. Say out loud right now in this moment, "I feel confused and stressed often, not I am confused and stressed often" (or whatever feeling we're experiencing). When we say these things out loud, it helps lock them into our memory. The dual action of speaking and hearing ourselves has significant effects on the knowledge structures that ensure memory.

By using RemindHers and speaking them aloud, we are training our brains to understand what we feel as feelings and not who we are. We teach our brains to understand that this is what "we feel" and not who "we are." So, we feel overwhelmed (not we are overwhelmed), we feel stressed, we feel sad, we feel confused, not we are all of these things.

This leads us to an important discovery: feelings can be managed. When we stop treating our feelings as if they are our true selves and understand they are emotions, we can manage them in a healthy way to create a better life for ourselves.

Understanding our own emotions, also known as "intrapersonal emotional intelligence," is important for our overall well-being and helps us manage our emotions better. Here's why this matters:

- **Better Self-Awareness:** When we understand our own emotions, we can recognize how we feel in different situations. This self-awareness helps us understand what makes us happy, sad, stressed, or angry.
- **Improved Emotional Control:** Knowing our emotions helps us control them better. For example, if we know that certain things make us angry, we can learn ways to stay calm and not overreact.
- **Better Decision-Making:** Understanding our emotions helps us make better decisions. When we know how we feel, we can think more clearly and choose actions that are good for us and others.
- **Greater Well-Being:** Being in touch with our emotions can lead to a happier and healthier life. We can handle stress better and enjoy positive experiences more fully.
- **Effective Relationships:** Understanding our own emotions can also improve our relationships with others. When we know how we feel, we can communicate better and understand others' feelings too.

So, simple RemindHers and the practice of speaking aloud have real science behind them. They allow us to teach ourselves new habits to be the people we want.

We want to share ideas that help us cope more positively and powerfully because we are unbelievably beautiful, powerful spirits with so much wisdom on how to navigate through our lives, meant for great things even when we're navigating hard days. The way we feel will come and go along the way. It's important to know the difference.

What's Challenging You Right Now?

Often, the most difficult feelings come when life challenges us. We think challenges come when change is needed. Someone once asked us this powerful question: Why, on a really good day when things are going our way, do we have no problem feeling empowered in the belief that this is meant for us, but on the hard days, when life may also be guiding us in the right direction, why don't we have the same belief that these days are meant for us too? We think the magic lies within how we welcome the challenge and then welcome the change.

The good news is that the types of people like you who read books like this have already taken the first step in navigating through hard times. Just picking up this book (or downloading the eBook) proves you want to do something about this lost or challenging place you're in and figure out how to get unstuck. You're already ahead of the game. Congratulations on your search for the next steps in your journey.

We're willing to bet that when you think about your past, there are challenges that came before change, and you're here in this moment looking for something different in your life, needing something different, some kind of change to help you feel better or more connected to your purpose than you do now. Maybe you're searching for something that reignites the magic or power inside you that you may have felt as a young girl. Did you have something like Chrissy's magic words that used to help you dream?

While we believe words are magical, and that magic exists in the universe, we want to be careful to assure you that this book is not some magic cure. The magic cure for what is bothering you or holding you back lies within you. We can't wait to show you how to access it. Beautiful soul, you have all the power and magic that lives inside your unique spirit that you will need in your life. We know that at times you may not feel like you do and this book will B your RemindHer.

We don't need to know exactly what you're struggling with right now, though if we were sitting in front of each other in the lounge inside our family jewelry store, or across from each other at a coffee shop, we would absolutely hold that space for you to share. We would listen, and we would offer to sit with you in the hard stuff or celebrate the good things. Since in this moment we are connecting with this book, not in person, what we need is for you to read these words with an open heart and with your current struggle in mind. Our goal is to help you find more joy, especially in the hard times.

Over time and through life lessons, we now truly understand that humans were created to experience joy, and this book is, in part, the story of how we learned to live that in a modern world full of pressures that can make joy hard to prioritize. The very essence of your spirit is joy. We are personally reminded of this every time we hear our children laugh, or feel the goosebumps of pure purpose when we unveil a perfectly designed piece for a customer, or when we take that moment to tend to our garden or take a much-needed walk in nature. It doesn't matter what we're doing; the lilting sound of their laughter, the look on a customer's face, the feeling of peace on a hike is contagious joy, no matter what else is going on in our lives. We can't help but pause and smile.

Sometimes happy tears spring to our eyes in these types of moments, and we're reminded that joy is innocent, playful, creative, and requires a simple willingness to just be present in the moment. When life gets hard, we often get distracted and disconnected from that joy. We cannot let go; we cannot exist in the moment, and our brains go down the rabbit hole of stress, worry, or fear.

This is where self-care and Spirit-care come in. When we say self-care/Spirit-care, we mean taking care of your mind, body, and especially your spirit. We all hear about self-care constantly—but spirit-care is how you make space for joy.

Why all this talk about joy? Because joy is medicine for the spirit. When you connect to joy, you connect to your Power to B.

To explain, let's tell you a story.

Chrissy

The weekend before I was supposed to start writing this book, I found myself in the hospital having a panic attack. The irony of the fact that I was in the hospital dealing with anxiety just before writing a chapter about being fearless is not lost on me, but it's also the perfect way for me to introduce exactly what I mean when I talk about your Power to B (and to illustrate, that you *CAN* connect with your power, and maybe still find joy in the middle of that storm I mentioned earlier).

I sat there, hooked up to machines and waiting on tests to ensure that what I felt was panic and not an actual heart attack. I had ironically chosen my Bfearless bracelet that morning. I needed Bfearless on my wrist that day, touched it often, and relied on this physical reminder of who I am, what I'm capable of, and how I behave even in the face of fear. The bracelet is a tool I use. You may develop your own tools in the course of this book, in fact, I hope you do. What works for you may be different than what works for me or others. Or feel free to do exactly the things I share to get your momentum started. Developing your custom-designed, personally curated Spirit-care practice is the point of this book.

I'm sharing this story of my panic attack with you because before we move on, I need you to know this book, this framework, this brand is not about eliminating unpleasant feelings and emotions. This is about how to cope and B your best self possible on the good days, the hard days, and every day in between. It's about harnessing your Power to B and finding joy in the struggle over and over again.

Before we jump into the Powerwords, we want to remind you one more time. The Power to B is a daily practice of reminding yourself who you are, what you've been through, all you've accomplished, and how you can harness that energy to power through every day. You'll see this framework put into practice throughout this book as we tell you about each of the Powerwords we use to remind ourselves how we want to show up and what we set out to B each day. Our hope in sharing this is that you can take the parts that work for you, leave what doesn't and develop a mind, body, and Spirit Care practice to help you hold onto your joy, harness your power, and thrive through the storm.

RemindHer: You were created to experience joy.

CHAPTER 3:

Bfearless

---

*"Life is full of difficult obstacles, and there is
only one way through them."*

~LIZ CAVANNA

Chrissy

I am one of those people who is always on time or a few minutes early, but not this day. This day, back in 2011, I was rushed and running late. I hate being late, and that means sometimes I put a lot of pressure on myself (and those around me), pressure leads to stress, and . . . I just hate being late. This time, though, It meant I got to encounter something I wouldn't have if I wasn't paying attention. This morning, running late meant I got a sign that changed my perspective. On this morning I was preparing to go to the fertility clinic. Again. Anyone who's been through fertility challenges understands just how often you have to step through those doors and see breathtaking images of drooling babies all over the walls. I was stressing, and praying, and overthinking some more as I got ready for the day. I quickly grabbed my coffee cup for one last sip before heading out the door and splashed some on the sleeve of my shirt. I ran to the sink and pushed back my sleeve to wipe the stain, and my wrist tattoo, the same one I'd had for at least a decade, stood out like a smack in the face in that moment. Not literally, but it felt like it was trying to get my attention. On my wrist is a small tattoo that says faith. I got it once upon a time as a reminder to myself to keep the faith when life is hard (see, hindsight is 20/20 they say, and I've been using words as visual reminders long even before The Power to B was a thing).

That morning I was on my way to the fertility clinic for a blood test to see if our last round of intrauterine insemination worked. For those of you who don't know, IUI is a cringeworthy procedure where they take sperm and insert it directly into your uterus in the hopes that, if they make the whole situation easier for the swimmers, one of them is bound to find an egg and make you puke for several months. The whole process is weird, embarrassing, expensive, and totally worth it if you get to actually have a baby at the end.

Anyway, back to the tattoo smacking my face. This was our last attempt before we'd have to move onto in vitro fertilization, or IVF, the process where they make your baby in a petri dish and place an actual embryo in your uterus. It's weirder, and even more expensive than IUI, and I hoped we wouldn't have to go that far to become parents. My tattoo did its job that day, and helped by reminding me to center myself, take a breath, and walk out the door knowing that whatever the results of that blood test were, Danny and I would keep going on our determined path to become parents someday.

My tattoo was reminding me to never lose faith and remember that good things are meant for me. I stood there, leaning against the counter (and making myself even later) and remembered the way that tattoo made me feel before and why I got it in the first place. Seeing this tattoo on that day took me from "This is hopeless, it's never going to work and I'm nervous as hell" to "whatever is next is meant to be, Bfearless, stay faithful." With that reminder, I was able to feel hope and faith alongside the fear and move forward. I felt a renewed sense of hope, confidence, and a little less fear.

On my way to the clinic I kept thinking about how I had forgotten about faith during the process and the way fear and stress on my mind and body kind of took over. As I continued to think about the faith part and dialing it up going forward, I got goosebumps over my whole body while driving. Goosebumps are my indication of a sign of something good and to pay attention. I often get this feeling when things are headed in the right direction, even when I'm designing someone's custom jewelry or redesigning an heirloom pieces and hearing their story—goosebumps, tears stinging my eyes—I then get to creatively find a way to pull that emotion into the piece I'm designing.

I called Danny from the car.

"I got a sign," I told him. (I'm always telling him about the signs I receive.)

"What happened?" He never makes me feel silly for my belief in signs.

I told him about the tattoo. "I don't know what's going to happen. I don't know how but I know that even if it doesn't work this time, it will be okay."

"I want to get the same tattoo someday." He wanted to become a dad as much as I wanted to be a mom. I felt strengthened, knowing I had him on my side.

That appointment didn't go the way I'd hoped. I think a higher power was preparing me for that disappointment and reminding me to keep going, hold onto the faith, and know that things will work out. I would become a mother, one way or another.

My tattoo served as a visual reminder to stay the course, take action, and hold onto the faith that someday, somehow, I'd have someone call me mom. That experience, and several that came later, shaped The Power to B brand into what it is today. Our first Powerword was Bfearless.

Bfearless Means to Fear Less

We think it's vital to give you our definition of fear and fearlessness before we move on. We could tell you the proper definition from a dictionary, but we both know how words come to mean something different to each of us as we move through life and also does anyone even use a dictionary anymore? :)

Fear is not the protective instinct that is innate in all of us and kept our ancestors safe from direct threats to life. That fear is your brain trying to keep you alive and was especially important when a sharp toothed predator was bearing down on early humans as they ran for cover. This fear is not what we're talking about when we say fear in this chapter. This is not the fear that landed one of us in the hospital the day before we were to start turning this book's outline into an actual book.

The fear we want to chat with you about is the fear that will always be present when you strive for a goal or are trying to make a change. Whether you're training for a marathon, trying to parent sassy children, or creating a business that meshes your dreams together with your skills, there will be a little voice inside trying to tell you why you can't or shouldn't. Any time you try to grow, change, heal, or push through challenges, that voice will creep in.

Call it what you want—inner critic, the devil—the goal of that voice is to keep you small, keep you stuck, and keep you in a place where the familiar rules your life.

To Bfearless, then, is not the absence of fear. If that voice will always be there, we cannot outrun it, and if we try, we will fail and become pretty exhausted too. We know, we've tried. When we spent years trying to have children, and nothing seemed to work, we tried to ignore the fear. Doing that just made the fear grow until we thought we'd never be parents. It wasn't until the best quote we heard, we can't remember where: "the only way through is through." Fear ignored just grows stronger and louder. Our hope for you to embrace Bfearless is for you to take decisive action toward your goals and dreams, regardless of what fear tries to tell you to do (or not do).

Rae

Being fearless has many meanings. It can mean being adventurous or outgoing but for some of us, that isn't in the cards yet. For me, the first step to becoming fearless is to quite literally, fear less than I typically do. Enforcing this step only became a reality to me after bringing home a baby after struggling with infertility. To further this, my husband and I were sent home with a baby, and without a manual. (I know, it's shocking that they expect us to just be able to keep a human alive without a how-to guide.)

You can be around children all your life but when you leave the hospital for the first time with an actual human that depends on you, you wind up with lots of fear and feelings of anxiety. Shortly after coming home, I remember calling Chrissy with a million questions. How do I know when to feed the baby? How am I leaving this baby when I go back to work? What about sleep?

How often do babies eat? How long do they sleep for? How do I know if they are getting enough milk, how do I make this baby stop crying? Chrissy gave me the RemindHer I needed to breathe, be graceful, and stop fearing the unknown. I had to take things as they came and stop worrying about things that happened already or things that haven't even happened. She reminded me that there is no place being present in fear and there is no place for fear when you're fully present.

When I went back to work, I had a plan for childcare, but then I made a back-up plan. I had plan on top of plan on top of plan but I realized that being fearless meant letting go of my need to over plan. This need was keeping me away from the gratitude that is so important in our lives. Once I was able to master fearing less, I could finally start living more fearlessly.

Since then, I've learned so many more tools, like deep breathing, for managing anxious feelings. I've never been one to hold onto anxiety (though I have so much compassion for those who do), so starting my day focused on positivity and gratitude makes me start each day feeling lighter. Every day, I wake up before everyone else, work out, journal, cold plunge and drink some coffee. That's what I learned works for me through trial and error. Doing these things makes me feel like my best self. I decided that when I had the family I worked so hard for, I would be the best version of myself for me and for them.

Chrissy

As Danny and I moved through our infertility journey, I found fear creeping in, threatening to become my constant companion. When we both went for testing after a year of having fun and trying things on our own, the doctor called it unexplained infertility. I called it frustrating and unfair. When we tried medication, and each month nothing happened despite my ovaries producing what looked like healthy eggs, I asked, "What if I never become a mom?"

That fear turned to hopelessness, and to anguish—fear that cuts so deep you feel it in your bones. Brené Brown describes fear as anguish in Atlas of the Heart in this way, "Anguish not only takes away our ability to breathe, feel, and think, it comes for our bones. Anguish often causes us to physically crumple in on ourselves, literally bringing us to our knees or forcing us all the way to the ground. The element of powerlessness is what makes anguish traumatic. We are unable to change, reverse, or negotiate what has happened. And even in those situations where we can temporarily reroute anguish with to-do lists and tasks, it finds its way back to us."

Every time the clinic would call with the news that I wasn't pregnant, I already knew. The word on the street was they call the pregnant people in the morning and save disappointing people until mid-afternoon. My calls came in the afternoon again and again, and I'd find myself sobbing, feeling defeated each time on my knees, with the phone still in my hand. Anguish, hopelessness, powerlessness, fear.

That day my tattoo smacked me in the face, however, I still cried but I didn't crumple when I got the call. Even in the face of more bad news, another failed attempt, and further disappointing my husband, I knew I would be okay, and that what was next was meant for me.

This made me curious. What else can I do to prevent spending less time crumpling even when I was still crying into my phone?

I started writing and surrounding myself with positive affirmations, or Powerwords, on post it notes and placing them around my home, dry-erase notes on my bedroom mirror, on my cell phone lock screen, etc., so I could start my day with more faith and hope. I know that not getting pregnant wasn't my fault and that stress is not the only factor, but there is so much to B said about keeping your energy in a good place. I wanted to elevate my vibe, reduce my stress, and attract motherhood into my life instead of desperately chasing it in the dark.

This practice of leaving words as reminders is my go-to strategy, and so my sister and I decided to create Powerword jewelry. As a jewelry designer, I'm always looking for ways to make our daily practices more beautiful, and the idea for Powerword jewelry was a natural fit. Each day, I'd place a bracelet on my wrist and remind myself to feel the fear and do it anyway—to move forward because what is on the other side is worth it.

Two years later, I sat next to my husband at a tattoo studio just after leaving the doctor's office. He could finally get his faith tattoo. After a long, arduous journey and a few rounds of IVF, we heard our daughter's heartbeat on ultrasound. Months later, when Scarlet was born, our tattoos became not only a reminder to move through the fear, but a beautiful testament to what is possible when you keep the faith.

Carry Bfearless in Your Heart

This is our hope for you, that you learn to Bfearless and keep the faith. You will not outrun the tough situation you're in, nor would we want you to—what's on the other side of this situation is meant for you. What we want is for you to find a practice that helps you cope with anxiety, fear, and stress so that you don't wind up face-down on the floor every time adversity hits.

When was the last time you felt powerful? What were you doing? Were you holding tightly to control, or were you letting a higher power lead you in the right direction?

What are you afraid of right now?

How does fear feel in your body? Do your shoulders tense? Does your stomach turn over?

What do you do when fear creeps in? Do you run from it? Wallow in it?

What if, instead of running or wallowing, you could find a way to sit in the discomfort until you're calm and quiet enough to hear what the fear is really trying to tell you? What if you could decide to move forward on your goals even when fear laughs at you?

The next time fear threatens to overtake you, pray for the clarity you need, be grateful for every fear you've overcome before, cultivate a feeling of hope to keep anguish at bay, take care of yourself (I mean it, go drink some water and have a snack), remind yourself what's worked before, and get curious about what new thing you can try to find joy in this particular season of fear. And for goodness' sake, keep track of all you've accomplished so you can remind yourself again and again what you're capable of when you look at fear, say "not today," and decide to do the hard thing anyway.

Bfearless Action Steps

- Acknowledge what you're afraid of.
- Spend some time fearing less in your current season. What can you let go of?
- Decide to lean into faith that the outcome, though it may not be what you hope for, will be what is meant for you.
- Take care of yourself even more than usual. Add in a bit more rest, some extra time with loved ones, or more

opportunities with your favorite hobby when you're facing something scary.
- Remind yourself of all the fears you've worked through before, and all that you've accomplished.

For more help with Bfearless, and the other Powerwords, we created a companion journal where we share my methods for working through life with Powerwords as a guiding force. In the journal, we help you keep track of your accomplishments, focus on gratitude, and find joy on the good days, the hard days, and every day in between. Get the journal here.

SCAN ME

> RemindHer: Bfearless means to fear less every day so you can more easily see opportunities for joy.

CHAPTER 4

Bfierce

---

*"Being a special needs mom, there are times when I have
to advocate for my child. Bfierce reminds me of my power."*

~K. BRAD

Remember your purpose and let it drive you. There's nothing you can't do.

Chrissy and Rae gifted me a Bfierce bracelet, and I'll never forget that moment! The three of us have bonded our friendship over many life experiences which unfortunately includes fertility struggles. These girls truly knew me and knew this bracelet and specifically the word fierce was going to be the daily reminder and affirmation I needed! Positive affirmations help change your mindset to get you through challenging times, Chrissy and Raeann have brought this to life!

~CHRISSY MONACO DIMAURO

Rae

Bfierce is your go-get-it zone: you put on the power shoes and go get the world. I used to be fierce all the time when I was becoming a very strong female entrepreneur with new goals. I would strap on my six-inch Louboutin heels and feel like I could rule the world. I now keep those shoes inside my closet, way up high as a reminder. May the days of wearing those heels rest in peace (wearing heels after having kids doesn't feel the same!). We all have a certain suit or dress or shoe that gives us our tigress energy and when we want to feel confident as he**, we put them on. Those are your roaring days... that's what Bfierce is.

As I've grown, I've learned to pace myself a lot better—back in the Louboutin days I went full steam ahead, all the time. Today, I've realized I have a higher purpose in my life and now, it's bringing on steady energy instead of power energy. big cat energy: power and then crash: now, I need steady consistent energy: always feel motivated, ready to go for the day but not need a big thing to happen every single week. It's unrealistic to maintain that level of power/tiger energy. I do still get the urge to power through and charge ahead at full speed, but now I know I need to get off the boat sometimes. I want to live at a consistent pace without all those peaks and valleys. I want to hit celebratory moments without having to then hit a valley afterward.

Chrissy

All of us have a shitty relationship under our belts (some of us are still in it. Don't worry, you will be okay. Find the strength to leave and trust the future you to figure out the details). In my twenties, I found myself entangled in a relationship that was nothing short of toxic. I don't want to get into details, because people who hurt us don't deserve that much air time, but I'll briefly describe him with a series of stark terms: manipulative, narcissistic, an addictive gambler, and unfortunately, much more. It was a draining five-year experience and leaving demanded a level of courage I didn't know I possessed.

Leaving required me to Bfearless, but staying away and rebuilding my life required me to Bfierce. I rebuilt my credit, paid off debt, moved back in with my parents, and made a life that helped reconnect me to myself. I couldn't yet think about dating without wanting to throw up a little bit, so I got a dog and named him Rubicon (Ruby for short) after the most powerful river in Greece. I needed a little extra power in my life as a reminder that I needed to Bfierce.

Bfierce is about grabbing hold of the momentum gained from taking that initial brave step (the one you took when you were using Bfearless). When doubt creeps in (and it will), being fierce means pushing forward and maintaining the progress you've started. Bfierce requires you to recognize that obstacles and struggles are a normal part of life. Bfierce asks you to commit to every day, asking yourself, "What's one thing I can do today for potential progress?" Bfierce is a mindset which underlines the truth that if it were easy, everyone would do it—Bfierce acknowledges that challenges are inevitable, but it's how we face them that defines our journey. The only guarantee in life is that everyone will face challenges, but not everyone will choose to Bfierce in confronting them.

Ruby and I settled into a comfortable dog and dog-mom relationship. His tiny Yorkie body would shake as he greeted me after work each day, and I found solace in the quiet evenings I spent at home with him as my cuddle-buddy. Ruby helped remind me what happiness felt like, and his presence was a gentle reminder that love does not have to be so complicated.

I was happy, comfortable with myself, and thought I could start dating again (without the urge to throw up).

Then, I met Danny and had to call on Bfierce in a whole new way. (If you've already read Chapter 1, you know Danny and I wind up married but remember, at this point, I met him and didn't know how it all worked out, so stick with me.) Bfierce is one of the driving forces behind mine and Danny's marriage, so it makes sense that I needed Bfierce to even start our relationship.

When I met Danny, I thought I was ready, but in reality, I was too scared I would repeat the patterns that landed me in the toxic relationship years before. I held back, and refused to make myself vulnerable. I didn't respond to his messages because I didn't yet trust myself.

Luckily, Danny was persistent. A few weeks went by, and Danny reached out again. This pattern of him reaching out, and me withdrawing lasted for a while. It took a few months for me to say yes to a date.

I had to Bfierce to say no when I wasn't ready, and Bfierce to say yes to starting the relationship despite my fear that I'd end up in another toxic situation. **What it means to Bfierce will change based on where you are, what you need, and what you're working toward**.

Fast forward several years, many dates, a wedding, and IVF journey and Danny and I found ourselves squarely back in the Bfierce space. As we approached our fifteenth anniversary Danny and I hit that spot all marriages hit at some point. We were a bit bored, and going through the motions. We'd both gained some weight, and at the risk of coming across as superficial, I decided I needed to mention it to him. My concerns were more about our overall well-being—his low energy, the dullness in our relationship, and our physical and mental health, but physical attractiveness matters in a long-term relationship too.

We decided to liven things up while addressing our out-of-shapeness and train for a marathon. (Yes, I know that's a bit crazy, you might choose something else, and that's just fine.) My point is that choosing to do something new and difficult requires you to Bfierce.

When I shared our plan to train for a marathon with people they asked why or expressed doubt. The same will probably happen to you when you work to Bfierce in moving toward your goals. The doubt may come from well-meaning family and friends who love you.

Don't leave your secure job to chase your entrepreneurial dreams, it's not safe. Why would you want to travel alone? Aren't you worried about safety? Are you sure you want to marry them?

Just because the people delivering this advice love you doesn't mean the advice is something you need to listen to. You aren't chasing this dream for them, or anyone else, you're doing it because you want to. You know when it's the right thing, and trust your intuition… It will be hard some days, but you can absolutely do this. Whatever you're working toward, you know when it's right. This thing you're trying fills your soul to bursting and ignites a fire in your belly. When you're fueled by passion the path isn't necessarily easy, but there is a rhythm to it, and a constant feeling of alignment. Don't give it up just because someone says you should. Trust your intuition and Bfierce.

On the other hand, if you're striving for a goal for the wrong reasons, or because it's what someone else thinks you should do, the path will be much more difficult. You'll drag yourself out of bed every morning, and then have to pull yourself through most of the day. You'll accomplish things, but you won't get the same thrill from it. If that's where you're at right now, we want you to know it will be okay. You can find a way to leave the shoulds behind and do more of what you want to be doing with your life. It starts with a decision.

When Danny and I decided to train for a marathon together, it was because we were living in that stuck place. A marathon may seem like a strange choice, but I'd argue that any hard thing we decide to do feels a bit like a marathon. Starting a business, raising children, building a marriage, buying a house, paying off debt, and so many other things you decide to accomplish will be more like a marathon than a walk in the park. You'll need to commit to taking that first step, remind yourself why you're doing this thing, and sometimes you'll need to push yourself a bit harder. You'll also need rest, and fuel, and connection to yourself and your higher power. Some days the run will feel easy, and other days you'll run uphill in a downpour and your water bottle will spring a leak just after the sole on your sneaker comes loose. If you're committed, however, those hard days will be a little easier because your why will drive you to take that next step, floppy sole be damned.

This commitment to Bfierce in our marathon training led to what I describe as the zero-nine mile conversation. This morning session was our longest training session to date. So much emotion about our lives, the state of our marriage, and everything we were struggling with bubbled up during our ride to the starting point. We pulled into the park, both crying, exhausted, and feeling a bit like a washcloth that's been soaked, wrung out, and tossed into the corner of a hotel shower.

I had Bfierce on my wrist. I touched the bracelet, and remembered why we'd started this training in the first place. I looked at Danny, and he nodded. (This is one of the beautiful parts of marriage—when he knows what I'm thinking without me saying a thing.)

"Let's just get out and run to the end of the block." I knew that if we took that first step we'd remember why we started this journey and we'd find a way to carry on.

Our feet struck the pavement, tears still drying on our cheeks as we ran that first block. Then we ran the first mile. Then the first four. Our lungs burned, our legs grew weak, and we thought about giving up more than once. Eventually, we finished all nine miles of that run. Then we did it again. We spent the next months getting up at crazy hours, running in the dark, and keeping Bfierce in the back of our minds.

Six months later, in May 2023, we ran the Providence Marathon in Providence, RI. We've used the same momentum-building strategy when we decided, after reading Smart Couples Finish Rich to move toward a debt-free life, when we decided to revive our dating life with at-home date nights every Wednesday, and for a number of other goals over our decades together.

Bfierce also requires some flexibility and a willingness to surrender control. Some goals took a year longer than we planned. Life has a way of throwing a wrench into the best-laid plans, and when you're raising a family and building careers, those wrenches seem to come one after another. How do you hang in there when things don't go as planned? At the end of the day, you have to remember that the timeline of your goals it's not entirely up to you. You can set your goals and work toward them, but we believe that you have to surrender, release control, and believe that there is a higher power taking care of the rest.

Bfierce While Taking Care of YOU

Another vital part of Bfierce is to take care of yourself along the journey. This is the Spirit-care we've mentioned before. You have to ensure that you're well fed, well hydrated, but also that you're having fun and enjoying life along the way. Don't get so bogged down in your goals that you lose sight of what life is all about—living.

We once traveled to see Rachel Hollis in Boston, and a woman in the audience stood up and said she wanted to lose twenty pounds as her goal. Hollis asked her what she was going to do once she lost the weight. "I'm gonna go to the beach, wear shorts, and have an ice cream." Hollis asked the woman why she wasn't going to the beach, wearing shorts, and eating ice cream now. You do not have to wait to experience it.

Bfierce in pursuing that goal, but have some fun right now!

Chrissy

If you're always waiting until you have the "perfect body" before you enjoy life, you will wait forever. I had a full metamorphosis in my twenties and thirties, and now, in my forties, I'm going through it again. I can't wait to see what changes my fifties bring. Every woman around you is going through this too—maybe not at the same time, but it's time to start talking about these changes. If you follow people on social media or have friendships with people who are telling you that their life is perfect and they never go through hard seasons, unfollow them, or set some boundaries up in the relationship to protect yourself. Go right now, and unfollow anyone who makes you question your worth or feel uncomfortable, unfollow them. Go, I'll wait.

I understand the mentality that makes women say, "When I lose weight, I'll be happy, buy the dress, etc." I grew up with the "I have to be on a diet" mentality. I have been on a diet since I was a teenager. If I weighed a certain amount, it would be a good day, if I was heavier, it was a bad day. I let the scale dictate how I felt for too long. There will be days when you don't move toward your goals. You will fail that day. You will stay in bed instead of going to the gym, you will buy Starbucks instead of saving, and you will wallow in self-pity instead of taking steps to turn your career into something you love. It's okay. Just don't kid yourself about it, take the rest consciously, and understand that you're making the decision to rest so you don't end up in the hospital with a panic attack because you burn yourself out. You have a full plate; some things will topple off the edge.

I call bull on the idea that you'll be happier when you're twenty pounds lighter. I applaud anyone working on health and wellness goals because you want to be stronger and healthier because you love to dance, or lift weights, or run. But, please, don't deny yourself joy because you think your thighs are too big. Be happy now, and celebrate that you CAN do these things, there are a lot of days between now and the goals you have in mind . . . wouldn't you rather look back and say I was happy every day along the way?

Besides, if you don't take stock of the day-to-day changes, and the tiny bits of transformative magic, you'll miss out. The magic of what happened when I ran a marathon wasn't the marathon itself, it was the palpable change in my marriage that occurred along the journey of training for the marathon. This has been true for any goal I've ever crushed. The accomplishment of the goal isn't magical. What you learn about yourself when you're fearless enough to take the first step, and fierce enough to stay the course is the secret sauce. Those are the things you'll look back on in your accomplishments list and think, "hell yes, I did that!" The magic is in the tiny details.

The other incredible thing that happens when you integrate Bfierce into your life is that other people notice what you're doing too, and then you get the bonus of inspiring others. Your daughter will see you taking care of yourself and know that she can take care of herself too. She will see you running full speed into the ocean and know that women get to have fun. The younger women in your office will see you making career changes and decide to embrace what they truly want too. Your partner will see you lace up your sneakers, even when it's raining, and decide to put theirs on as well.

That's the secret of Bfierce—when you do it right, others notice too.

So, remember why you started, keep that momentum, know that challenges will come, rest and care for yourself when you need to, and have some fun along the way. Whatever you do, though, don't dare give up. Get up tomorrow and put your floppy-soled sneaker on the pavement, refill your water bottle, and keep training. You've got a life to live.

What Gets in the Way of Bfierce

"I'm tired." Often, you're not truly tired; it's a mental state. The sooner you move past feeling tired, the sooner you can focus on bigger and better things. Dwelling on that tired energy keeps you stuck and makes you feel even more exhausted. If you're drinking enough water, getting sufficient sleep, and eating well, stop telling yourself you're tired. Instead, shift your mindset to: "I am acting as I should be right now."

Today, choose to be energetic. Choose to be thoughtful about where you direct your energy. By reframing your thoughts, you can change your perspective. For example, instead of saying, "I'm so tired," or "I feel like a bad mom," or "I'm so busy," try saying, "I feel tired or "I feel like a bad mom." This puts you in a mindset of fixing the problem rather than being stuck in it. When you say, "I feel tired," it becomes a catalyst for figuring out what you need—whether it's food, water, rest, or movement.

Rae

In my house, with two parents and three kids, it's okay for certain days to feel hard. But remember, there are always people in this world who, on your worst day, would consider it their biggest blessing. It's okay to have a day, week, or season that feels difficult, but try to refrain from saying, "My life is so hard." Learn to enjoy the ups because there will be downs. Embrace the good moments when they come.

> RemindHer: You deserve more power
> and more joy in your life.

CHAPTER 5

Blimitless

A reminder to not limit myself to what I'm capable of. Don't hold back! Show the world what I have to offer personally and professionally every [dang] day! When challenge creeps in, I feel empowered seeing my reminder that "there is no limit for me to push through and push forward.

—XO ANASTAZIA

Rae

It was around the age of five that I knew I was going to be in a leadership position. It was deeply ingrained in me that I was going to challenge perspectives and people—I would be in charge. I had thought I might be a lawyer, a CFO, or a designer. The jobs themselves changed over the years, but I always knew I'd be in a creative space and in charge of my own life. As adults we lose the freedom to have the creative thoughts that our child-selves used to have. Eventually, I knew I was going to write a book and be a *New York Times* bestseller, but I always thought it would be children's books.

Thinking about what your childhood self wanted will help you tap into the essence of who you are instead of the roles you play. Those will change.

There's a simple and profound truth in life: You are here to follow your passion and chase those dreams with all your heart. Your potential knows no bounds, and you are capable of incredible things.

Somewhere deep inside, you already know this. You may struggle to feel it, but it's there. That is why you set goals, strive for better, and seek to create a beautiful life. That's why you picked up this book.

Sometimes, though, setting goals can feel overwhelming. Have you ever sat in a room and been asked to set SMART goals? All of that realistic, time-bound talk can take some of the fun out of dreaming, can't it? Setting goals should feel like dreaming, but sometimes we put so much pressure on ourselves it loses its luster. The goals don't have to be big because in life, we make small goals every day. Yesterday was a day where I did all the things, I ended up over-doing everything because I was preparing for vacation. While yesterday felt intense start to finish, I treated myself and my family to not cooking dinner and just picking up takeout. This is rare for me because I pride myself on making healthy meals for my family. I said, "Self, let's reel it in, you can still be a hero even if you don't cook dinner tonight." My goal, usually, is to cook dinner every night, but sometimes we have to put less pressure on ourselves.

At some point, goal setting starts to feel like standing at the foot of a mountain, unsure where to begin. It can feel exhausting before we begin, but it's not as complicated as it seems. There is a way to make this journey a delightful one, feeling light and full of inspiration. There's a way to start dreaming again.

When you let go of the intense and heavy nature of goal setting, and embrace your Blimitless life, it can lead to a moment of clarity. It brings you to a place where you can make decisions with courage and conviction and be excited to take the first step—asking your future self for guidance. I could have let my day take all of my energy, but my future self deserves it too, and my kids deserve to absorb that energy from me. My kids need me to be the mom that is consistent—I have to walk into the house, release the stress of the day, hug my kids and be where my feet are.

Learning Blimitless

Chrissy

As I slip on my "Blimitless" bracelet, I can feel it. Blimitless is my connection to that little girl who thought that the nonsense words she wrote in the back of the station wagon could create mystical beasts and magical worlds outside her window. That bracelet is a symbol of unwavering belief in myself and a sense of liberation. I let it remind me that success isn't about shouldering the burden alone. It's not about toughing it out and overcoming the struggle. It's about trusting in yourself and the journey you're on. It's about believing in your own magic.

So, let me offer you these words of encouragement. Uncertainty will come, but there's a guiding light within you. When Rae and I started The Power to B jewelry collection, I often found myself questioning when the jewelry would sell, and if the idea would work. But, I used Blimitless as a reminder not to let myself be hemmed in by worry. Don't let the fear of the unknown dim your vision. Let your light shine. Let it show you the path ahead, revealing the limitless potential in your life. There's no stopping when you embrace that potential.

I want us to walk together in that light. Together, let's make this journey of spirit and purpose. You are capable of greatness—your own unique brand of greatness. What is your dream? What did you do as a child in order to connect with your magic? What did you want to do when you grew up? How would that little girl feel about who you are today? Would she smile at you and say " I knew you could do it," or would she remind you that it's time to get back to building her dream? The light within you is unique to your dreams, and with each step forward, you're one step closer to realizing all you imagined.

Your First Steps

Believing in yourself is the first step to Blimitless. Your dreams begin with belief. When Danny and I decided to run a marathon despite never having done so before, we began with an unwavering belief in our own power and ability to do the hard things.

Sometimes Danny needed me to remind him of his limitless potential, and sometimes I needed him to remind me as I bent over trying to catch my breath on a cold February training run.

I believed this so strongly that I got a tattoo to commemorate the accomplishment—not after the marathon—before the race even happened. I knew so deeply I would accomplish this goal that I was able to celebrate it before it happened and find motivation in the victory. Now, I had no choice but to finish. There was no backing down. With my new tattoo, I had claimed the victory, and now it was time to live it out.

There were moments when I questioned whether I had what it takes. You will have those moments too. Uncertainty will sneak in, but that little girl who believes in your power won't want you to give into it, and neither do I. If you're lucky you'll have someone, a friend, a brother or sister, or a lover who can cheer you on, or maybe you're going it alone right now. I want you to encourage yourself. Write phrases on post it notes and paste them all over your home. It may seem silly when you do it, but in those tough moments a little bit of self-encouragement goes a long way. In fact, when you're facing what seems like an impossible challenge, it might be all you have. Luckily, it's all you need to keep going.

The next step is to break it down into manageable pieces. Running the marathon is not about running the marathon. It's about running one mile. You run one mile at a time, one step at a time. Then you run five miles, then ten. Little by little, those miles become ingrained abilities. What once seemed impossible appears on the horizon. It comes closer and closer until it is in your grasp. Then, the next monumental task appears. Eventually, those single miles add up to crossing the finish line of your marathon. (Feel free to replace marathon with any challenge you're working on right now.)

The experience of training for and running that marathon together also led me to do something special for Danny on our anniversary. I wanted to make it unforgettable. So, I crafted a custom necklace for him, with two mountains standing side by side. It symbolized our shared journey of conquering challenges together. Engraved on the back were the words "15 years married." It was a symbol of love, endurance, achievement, and the triumph of taking one step at a time together.

These kinds of achievements are beautiful events, but they go beyond the moment in time. They have lasting effects that impact other areas of your life. Before sitting down to pen this chapter, Danny was grappling with self-doubt over something he's working through, so I gently reminded him: "Remember, you ran a marathon."

One achievement leads to another. Climbing one mountain gives the confidence you can climb the next. It begins with belief, and nothing builds that belief like the knowledge that you have achieved before. We look back at our triumphs as reminders of the strength and resilience within us. It's always there, waiting to guide us on the next monumental journey.

Perfect Is Not the Goal

Let's be real—chasing our dreams isn't always a picture-perfect journey. It's messy, challenging, and sometimes even ugly. That's OK. In spite of it all, there is beauty in the imperfection.

Remember, your goal is like a mountain—a large, daunting, unyielding mountain. You may need to climb the rocks, sludge through the mud, or tear through the thick brush. Despite it all, you can climb that big, beautiful, majestic mountain. Whatever the challenges, with each step forward, you're one step closer to reaching its peak. So keep going, one step at a time, and eventually, you'll conquer that mountain and stand triumphantly at its summit.

The Power of Imagination

Are you seeing it? Can you imagine your mountain's summit? Can you envision your finish line? Whatever your dream is, can you see it as a reality in your mind?

Your imagination is powerful. Allow yourself to dream freely and visualize the life you want. Set aside time to practice visualization. It's like nourishing your soul. Every time we're working toward something we spend time alone picturing ourselves accomplishing this goal. We've done this so often that now, when we talk about my future self or the goals we want to achieve, we have the habit of talking about it in present tense, as if we've already accomplished it. Those dreams of yours are not just fantasies. They're seeds waiting to blossom into reality. Keep nurturing them with your imagination, dedication, and hard work, and before you know it, you'll see them sprout into existence.

This is an invitation to explore, to grow, to discover, and to find your Blimitless life. You are capable of achieving greatness, but it all starts with your desire. It means keeping that intense desire to turn your dreams into realities through the power of your imagination.

Be True to Yourself

To live Blimitless, it's crucial to maintain self-awareness and honesty as things unfold. Life is unpredictable. It won't always go as planned. New opportunities will emerge. Distractions will be constant. You will learn new things as you go. As life unfolds, stay aware of your goals and make sure they are still aligned with your desires. Sometimes the goal you thought was worth chasing becomes something you no longer want or need.

It's an interesting balance to achieve. Chasing your dreams requires sacrifice, determination, and lots of hard work. You need strength, resilience, and focus to make it happen.

At the same time, you can't just keep your head down and drive forward. Sometimes, you need to pause for a moment and reflect. Decide if that goal truly is what you want. What sacrifices are you willing to make to attain it? Be honest with yourself and understand your own motives. Are you pursuing this goal for yourself, or are you merely chasing after the shadow of someone else's success? It's easy to get caught up in someone else's expectations. Blimitless people stay true to themselves, aware of their motives, and realize their desires.

Sometimes Blimitless means saying no to things that aren't quite in alignment, or quitting things that no longer fit your custom-curated life to make room for what was truly meant for you. Let us tell you about the time we tried to get our Power to B jewelry collection featured on QVC.

After our initial meeting with them, The goal looked achievable and we thought this was the path to launch The Power to B to the next level. we could imagine our jewelry being displayed there and the sales that would come as a result. The people connected with QVC loved the product and the branding, they loved the message. But they wanted our products to be cheaper. They pushed us to find a way to lower the price which would have meant changing the materials, or lowering costs in some other way. This began three years of meetings and check-ins to see where things stood. Eventually, once the process became so difficult we could no longer ignore the lack of alignment, we had to back out. We put in all the work to make that dream come true, but in the end, we had to be true to ourselves. We knew our pricing was fair, and we wouldn't compromise quality. We had to be true to The Power to B. Ultimately, we decided QVC was not something that aligned with our brand. This opened up space in our life and in our business for new ideas and a different direction.

It was not the victory that we originally imagined, but it was a victory nonetheless. Being true to yourself is always a win and a big part of your Blimitless life. Today, many people, including celebrities, wear Power to B jewelry. It didn't happen as we expected, but it happened, and we stayed true to ourselves in the process.

What goals have you pivoted on? What have you quit because you realized it no longer aligned with who you want to be? Is there something you're working toward right now that feels out of alignment in some way?

Think about Others

Here's a little secret: when you uplift others, you elevate your own spirit. A Blimitless life is not just about yourself. Empowering others is a source of energy. When it becomes your practice to inspire, empower, or uplift someone else, energy flows back into your life, filling you with vitality.

For me, and for many parents, the ones that we want to inspire most are our children and future generations. It's not enough to tell our own children they can follow their dreams. They need to see it lived out in our life. Inspiring, empowering, and uplifting our children is the greatest dream for us as mothers.

Chrissy

My son Kash takes Tae Kwon Do and it was time for him to attempt chopping a board in half. He was nervous, but he embraced his limitless capabilities. When he was able to chop a board in half with his bare hands I took the pieces and framed them, added "I can do it" written on them and hung it on the wall at the foot of his bed . That sign is the last thing he sees as he goes to bed every night. He's embracing his Blimitless self because he sees me do it every day as well.

Rae

Each day, set your mind to look for opportunities. Find your chances to encourage someone. It might be as simple as bringing a smile to someone's face. Giving is not a drain. There is a huge return on what you give. The more you give, the more you receive the energy and inspiration that ignites your soul.

Embrace Your Blimitless Life

Bfearless guides you in defining your goals and taking that initial leap. Bfierce propels you forward, building momentum with every stride. Now, Blimitless calls for reflection.

Blimitless moves us to eliminate self-doubt. The only barriers that exist are those in our minds. Everything is possible, but we are not trying to achieve everything. Your energy needs to be directed toward what truly sets your soul on fire.

Discernment Is Key

Discovering your true desires is the cornerstone. It's not about achieving goals for the sake of it. It's about aligning your actions with your deepest passions and finding what resonates with who you are.

This can be a powerfully inspiring process, but be aware that it becomes a struggle when we start to look at our already busy schedules. It's important to understand that we're not advocating for more than is already on your plate. Blimitless is exactly the opposite.

It's not about overscheduling; it's about discernment. A big part of the reflection process is eliminating what no longer serves you to make room for what matters. It's time to stop being busy and start being limitless.

Chrissy

Since I started working in our family business at sixteen years old, I have worked on weekends. It seemed like what I needed to do to build more business and grow in my career. Many years later and over time, and after both children were around two and five years old, I realized this practice did not align with my values.

I have more than one dream. I want to help build thriving businesses, but I also love my family and needed more time together. I needed to reflect on my goals and discern what needed to be in my schedule.

This reflection made it clear that working weekends did not align with who I am. I needed more time with my family. So, now I've learned to say "no" to weekend appointments. When I feel pressure to get work done, I remember the time I lost in the past and the regret I feel. That keeps me aligned with my goals. Overscheduling is not going to bring us to Blimitless. It takes discernment.

Celebrate Your Victories

The roadmap to your dreams lies in what you've already done. The Blimitless life is a journey of celebration—a celebration of your achievements, both big and small. Our reflection is not only about motivation and goals but also about being highly aware of all the victories along the way.

Chrissy

Five years ago, I took the first step on this path, driven by a burning desire to move to new heights in my career. It was a time of transformation, and I embraced the challenge of rebranding the power within me. I wanted to shape my career as a jewelry designer. Immediately, I started experiencing the fear of change and the weight of making these major life decisions. Despite the fear in my heart, I made a choice not to succumb to paralysis. I would not let fear stop me. I made a clear decision to stand tall and forge ahead.

To help me stay the course, I began by crafting a handwritten list in a small notebook of my proudest accomplishments. The list began with my children, the journey of fertility, and every hurdle I've overcome. Every entry served as a reminder of the miracles that come into our lives when we keep the faith. As I reflected on my biggest accomplishments, I found my inner guide to take me out of the darkness of fear. I began finding light in my victories.

Then, I moved on to any other accomplishments I could think of big and small. I was reminded of my resilience, strength, and belief in my potential. It became a journey of empowerment, overcoming the weight of doubt and embracing the possibilities ahead.

So, let's kick off your list of accomplishments with a celebration of all the wonderful things you've achieved. Don't try to say you don't have any. We know you do. There's no room for self-doubt here. You've accomplished more than you realize, and it's time to acknowledge and celebrate every triumph.

Here's a glimpse of just a few of the incredible feats you may have achieved:

- **Keeping Calm with the Kids:** You kept your cool and didn't lose your temper with the little ones. Celebrate showing patience and kindness to yourself and your family.
- **Date Day with Your Love:** You took the initiative to plan a daytime date with your spouse. You are nurturing your relationship and creating beautiful memories together.
- **Lifting Spirits with Friends:** A lunch date with a friend lifted your spirits and filled your heart with joy. Your ability to nurture friendships is commendable.
- **Family Fun Game Night:** Playing games with your kids brought laughter and joy into your home. Cherish these moments of pure, unadulterated fun.

- **Conquering the Inbox:** Learning how to use Google Drive is evidence of your willingness to embrace new skills and technologies.
- **Courageous Conversations:** You showed courage to engage in a difficult conversation, showing strength and appropriate vulnerability.

These are just a few possibilities. Think about it and make your list. Remember, sometimes your accomplishments are about trying new things, even if you decide you never want to do them again. Whether taking an arctic plunge or experimenting with new culinary experiences, each encounter shapes us and teaches valuable lessons.

If you want to feel motivated, learn to celebrate. Celebrate the moments that define you and draw inspiration from the challenges you've conquered. From celebrating each triumph, you will find the courage to leave behind the shadows of doubt and step into the brilliance of your Blimitless future. And always keep your ongoing list of accomplishments nearby. This is something we are currently working on!

Recognize Limiting Beliefs

You get to decide the conversation that takes place in your mind. You have the power to shine a light on your limiting beliefs and replace them with empowering thoughts that fuel your journey. When that voice whispers doubts in your ear, gently remind yourself of your history of accomplishments. Keep following that trail of victory, and know you are capable of achieving anything you set in your mind.

Limiting beliefs seek to stop you, but you have the power to think for yourself. You can recognize those negative thoughts and see the truth—those negative thoughts are wrong about you.

Let's look at some limiting beliefs that you may experience and how to address them:

- **You should meet other people's expectations.** Wrong. There is the temptation to shrink yourself to fit into someone else's mold. Resist that temptation. Embrace your authenticity and uniqueness. That is what matters most. Those who truly matter will appreciate you for who you are. Remember, it's not about blending in. It's about standing out, shining brightly, and living out your Blimitless life.

- **You should not want more in life.** Absolutely not. Your dreams are valid and worth your energy. You have every right to want more. Don't limit yourself. Allow your ambition and vision to overflow.

- **You should avoid doing things that may result in criticism.** Nope. American financier and adviser to U.S. Presidents Woodrow Wilson and Franklin D. Roosevelt, Bernard M. Baruch said, "Those who mind don't matter, and those who matter don't mind." Worrying about criticism will only hold you back and never help you. Surround yourself with people who uplift and support you, and let their encouragement drown out the noise of negativity.

- **You shouldn't try if you might fail.** Not a chance. Who said it was a failure? Part of the process is adapting, learning, and developing. Don't forget the power of letting go. Recognize when certain goals or endeavors are no longer serving you, releasing them to make room for new possibilities. That takes immense courage and wisdom. What some call failure can simply be learning experiences that help guide you in your Blimitless life.

Embrace your true self unapologetically. You are a dreamer, a visionary, and that's a beautiful thing. Embrace your ability to visualize your dreams and let it guide you towards your most fulfilling life.

Banish that negative voice and replace it with empowerment in your mind and the people around you. You are capable, worthy, and destined to live out your dreams. Believe it, embrace it, and watch as the world opens up to you in Blimitless possibility.

Keep Dreaming

If you've journeyed this far with us, it's because a spark within you yearns to ignite, to uncover what truly sets your soul on fire. What is it that you want deep down in your heart?

That dream is still within you, even if it has grown quiet over the years. For too many people, the art of dreaming has faded into the background. The demands of daily life soak up energy and squash the stirring of ambition. Yet, that spark of imagination still flickers within you. It's never too late to rekindle those flames.

Perhaps you were never taught how to dream. We can relate to that. It was something we had to learn as adults. Growing up, our parents instilled in us a strong work ethic, but the concept of dreaming seemed foreign. It wasn't until later in life, in our thirties, that we stumbled upon the magic of envisioning a life beyond the ordinary.

Discovering the ability to dream was like finding a hidden treasure. It became an exhilarating journey of self-discovery. Suddenly, the world was brimming with possibilities, and we were the architects of our destinies.

Now, it can be your time of exhilarating possibilities. It's time to unleash your imagination and embrace the thrill of envisioning a future filled with unlimited potential.

Chrissy

One day, a remarkable woman stepped into our store with a glimmer of determination in her eyes. She shared her desire to craft a ring symbolizing the boundless love she's committing to herself from this moment forward. Despite her inner turmoil stemming from an unfulfilling job, there was a quiet strength within her. I saw resilience waiting to be reignited.

We spoke of seeking clarity and guidance through whatever form speaks to her soul. Then, we discussed the magic of reminiscing about moments of pure joy and excitement from the past.

She shared with me her love for themed parties and her passion for interior design. Her face lit up with newfound energy as she spoke. She was rediscovering a piece of herself that had been buried beneath the weight of monotony.

As she left our store, after I designed her beautiful and meaningful ring, a transformation unfolded before my eyes. Her spirit was ablaze with newfound purpose. It goes to show the power of self-discovery and what awaits when we reconnect with our passions.

Keep Dreaming Together

As we close this chapter, let's envision the boundless possibilities that await when you embrace your limitless potential. The one thing you can know for sure is there is a 100 percent guarantee that something will happen rather than nothing. The goal is to influence what happens in powerful and positive ways.

We often think about our journey with Power to B. Taking those first prototypes home, hanging them up, and beginning our daily practice was our modest start. It was a pivotal moment. When we reached for our Blimitless bracelet we felt a surge of empowerment running through us. It was the first bracelet we ever wore and remains a constant reminder of my limitless potential.

Chrissy

One day, my daughter Scarlet caught sight of the collection in my closet. With wide-eyed wonder, she asked to see it. As she gazed upon the bracelets, I could see her excitement. It was as if she had stumbled upon a treasure trove.

"OMGosh, Mommy, this jewelry is a dream that's real!" she said.

At that moment, I realized the profound impact of setting an example of limitless possibility for our children and those dear to us. Scarlet now understands that dreams can indeed become reality and that realization is priceless.

I took the opportunity to explain the word "Blimitless" to her and how important it is. When you believe in your limitless potential, there's nothing you can't achieve. I assured her that I would always believe in her and be there to remind her of her limitless capabilities.

I love being the person who encourages my daughter. We all need that. It is vital to have someone to confide in who will listen and encourage you to dream freely. It's essential to carve out that space where your aspirations can take flight and where your imagination knows no bounds.

If you don't have that now, be on the lookout. If you're searching for that supportive person in your life, be open to new connections. You never know where you might find a kindred spirit who shares your enthusiasm for dreaming big.

You can start with books and podcasts and start with us. We want to be people in your life that will inspire you. We want to encourage you and be people that will empower the dream within you. Others will come along, but by making this journey with us, you already have people in your corner who know that you can Blimitless. If you feel moved to do so, we invite you to email us today and tell us what your Blimitless dream is. We can't wait to hear from you.

> RemindHer: Break through self-imposed boundaries to realize your full potential.

CHAPTER 6:

Bopen

$$\boxed{\text{Rae}}$$

In my current life, I'm adapting to Bopen. This is part of my journey that's happening right now as I write this book with Chrissy. I'm into manifesting and believing in signs and the universe making things come full circle.

Recently, I was driving down to Lake George for a family vacation. I decided to play a game with the universe as I often do. I knew my husband, Evan, had a lot of work stress and I said, "Sometimes you have to just relax and know the universe has your back. Let's ask the universe for a sign that all the decisions you are making are the right ones so you can enjoy this trip and rest assured that the universe has your back." He laughed...and then he played along. He asked the universe to show him a sign of a golden lion to help him know he's on the right track so he could let things go and enjoy our vacation and Bpresent. Less than a half hour later, we'd forgotten the conversation and moved on to snacks, car entertainment games and kids etc. Soon enough, we drove past the MGM casino in Springfield, and a giant symbol of a golden lion on the front of a building appeared right in front of us as we came around a turn. It stopped us in our tracks. After seeing this, I just smiled as my husband said, "Okay, there was no mistaking that one!" It was because of this that I have just recently freed up headspace in my life in a way that I can Bopen. When you start to believe that, you can finally start seeing the signs the universe sends your way, that's when you can Bopen.

Asking the universe for what you want is a new thing for me as in my previous headspace I felt busy, bored, and exhausted. To Bopen you have to start taking care of your mental and spiritual self. If you are in a space where you're doing all the things and taking care of all the tasks, you're not spending time in a free-thinking flow state. You aren't setting aside time for yourself because you don't understand how important it is. When I became disciplined about writing things in my journal, allowing thoughts to flow and giving myself mental space, I started to understand the power of my thoughts. I came to know that my mental state and my thoughts had an incredible influence over my life. This isn't something you can decide to change and immediately see a result, though. It must become a habit.

Building a habit takes at least ninety days, so, if you struggle to Bopen, realize that we're all busy and listing all the tasks in your day as reasons you can't allow yourself a moment is an excuse. Settle into the fact that life is busy and you GET to drive your kids to camp where they GET to engage in a day full of activities while you GET to go to work. Everyone is busy. Get over it, it's called life. (I know this is hard advice to read, but I give it with love.) Give yourself some gratitude for the life you GET to live.

Chrissy

When I was in college, my friend Bridget and I were driving to my parents' beach house in Rhode Island. We were singing along to "Milkshake" by Kelis and enjoying the summer sun in the way of carefree college students on summer break. We were so engrossed in our fun, we got off at the wrong exit. We realized it as soon as we got to the bottom of the exit ramp, and, luckily, when the light turned green, we were able to go straight and jump right back on I-95. The next time we made that drive, we decided we needed to get off exit 88 again because it was lucky the time before.

Since that day, I've noticed the number 88 showing up in other ways, sometimes subtle, and other times like an anvil over my head. When 88 shows up in my life it means I'm heading in the right direction. I see it on receipts, license plates, road signs, everywhere. 88 showed up in the parking lot of the fertility clinic more than once on days I didn't want to go in for another blood test or scan.

I see the number 88, and recognize it as a sign because I'm open to the possibility. Does this seem a bit too woo-woo for you? I understand that. At some point in my life I was skeptical of things like signs and astrology too, but once I started leaning in, and allowing the universe to guide me, or reinforce the decisions I was making, I found so many benefits that I decided to try one more thing, and one more. (Remember what I said about being curious? Maybe this is a time you can remain curious. Keep reading and explore how Bopen can work for you.)

In the introduction I listed asking for clarity and guidance as one of the steps in my Power to B process. Bopen is all about that step of the process. Bopen requires you to quiet your mind, have faith that good things are meant for you, and surrender to the idea that things will always work out, just maybe not in the way you hoped or planned.

In life doors don't always swing wide open; sometimes they quietly unlock, waiting for us to notice the signs pointing straight at them and then muster up the courage to turn the handle and push on through. Hey, here is a sign for you, the door is unlocked, Bopen and come on in. Bopen invites you here to fashion a new mindset, one that is ready to welcome new possibilities, and experiences and embrace the unpredictable twists of life. Bopen is about opening up to new ideas, it's also about proactively preparing yourself to recognize and grab ahold of signs that may otherwise go unnoticed. See how I said go unnoticed? I said that because we get signs from the universe all the time. We all do. But do we pay attention to them? Do we see them? More importantly, do we accept them?

Bopen is your passage to possibility and enlightenment; it helps you to see the big picture, reality, how life truly is and can be what you want it to be. My hope for you in this chapter is to learn to understand and to Bopen to the signs, the gifts the universe gives you, the gifts sent letting you know you are on the right path. I want to see you light up when you realize the power of Bopen. Allow me to take you through personal stories, lessons learned, and why I choose to Bopen.

Bopen to Signs—They Are Gifts

Rae

The universe will take care of you when you put good into the world. No one who believes in manifesting and karma will doubt this. The universe allowed me to see that joining this book project was the right decision for me. This was proven on the day I had a conversation with Chrissy about joining this project. On that day, so many signs showed up. My grandmother showed up all over the place: she was telling me to go for it, to do it, Chrissy and I had the number eight all over the place, the name Maria (our ghost-writer's name) came up everywhere. My uncle was also in town visiting and last minute hopped into the car with us for an evening of swim lessons and ice cream.

On our drive home, my husband at the last minute turned and went a different direction than usual. We got stuck in unexpected traffic, and all of the sudden an opening showed itself to make a quick turn off the highway. We went for it, got off the exit, made a left to go home and there was the graveyard where grandma was buried. This is not a place we visit often and have never brought the kids there but in this very same moment, my curious little kids were asking about grandma. "Uncle Phil, do you know grandma lives in my heart now?" "Mom, where is grandma's actual body now?" I explained as best I could to my 3, 5 and 7 year old and then told them about how we have adopted the Jewish tradition of leaving a stone or quarter on a headstone when you visit someone's grave. My son Zane reached far into his pocket and said, "You mean like this quarter I just picked up on the sidewalk at the ice cream shop?" If this wasn't a sign for us to pull over and visit Grandmas grave, I don't know what is.

The universe is constantly helping us, on our best days and especially on our worst. We just have to Bopen to receiving the guidance. With faith, an open mind, an open heart, and a little change in perception we can start to see, name, and recognize the little or big signs we get. Signs can come in any forms. They can be physical objects, animals, songs, numbers, anything really. For me they come as numbers (88 to be exact), red cardinals, swooping hawks, ladybugs, or whatever I ask for. Yes! You can ask for signs, too! How cool is that!? Be as specific as you can. Ask for a yellow polka dot dress, a pink elephant, a certain song or anything you can imagine. When you least expect it, you'll see someone wearing a yellow polka dot dress or you will hear the song somewhere random. You ask and the universe will deliver.

To truly Bopen to possibilities, sometimes you need to start before you feel ready. This might sound crazy, but do we ever really feel ready for big changes, anyway? We can always come up with some reason why we aren't ready yet. You could be waiting forever if you don't just start now. Take a leap of faith because you never know what you could be missing out on waiting for the perfect timing (that doesn't exist).

Embrace the possibilities. True readiness often comes after you've already started. Action creates motivation and momentum, and motivation and momentum build confidence.

Starting before you think you are ready and Bopen to signs, you align yourself with the flow of life and invite a multitude of positive experiences and magical opportunities.

Being Open to Signs Requires . . .

Slowing Down

Chrissy

This seems simple, but it's not: you have to be quiet, have faith, and surrender. When I'm putting my jewelry on, it takes a little time (those damn clasps are tricky, I want to be the jeweler who creates the bracelet clasp that is easy to put on by yourself, but I haven't figured it out yet). When there's no one around to help, I have to lean my arm against the stack of jeans in my closet, and hold it at just the right angle so I can hook the damn thing myself. When I'm contorting my arm, I'm forced to slow down, and this is when I ask for guidance and signs.

Finding moments of stillness throughout your day will be beneficial. Pick a time of day when you have to slow down anyway, showering, driving, folding laundry, chopping vegetables, or anything other than watching a screen (that will hijack your mind like an attention-stealing ninja). In these moments of quiet, it's important to guide your thoughts positively.

Say you change your mind about what you want for lunch. In that instant, you can turn your car around and head to a different spot to eat. You should be able to shift your thoughts in a new direction just as easily, right? While it may not be easy at first, it will become a valuable practice you will soon appreciate. It won't happen instantly—just as you can't decide you want to go to Aruba and teleport yourself to the beach right now. Anything worthwhile takes time and practice, one quiet moment at a time.

If you are finding it challenging quieting your mind, it is okay to seek help or guidance and to stack the tools and develop strategies that work for you. Don't be afraid to try different things. Maybe you can find solace in hiking, or working out, maybe taking a quiet walk or drive can help you shut it off. You can try talking to a trusted friend or finding a relatable therapist can help you find your unique recipe for what works. Let's be honest. You will need to stack a few tools in your toolbox for those extra challenging times.

When I experienced a full blown panic attack shortly after starting this book, my head was spinning, but I reminded myself that everything happens for a reason. After leaving the hospital and picking up my prescription with Danny, I realized my panic attacks were partly related to my monthly cycle. My doctor prescribed Xanax as a backup for my overwhelming moments. I have to say that as I'm working hard and learning some amazingly powerful holistic coping mechanisms for managing stress, just knowing I have it on hand helps me stay more balanced, knowing I have a solution if I need it. To be honest, I had thought about asking for a prescription before but I hesitated because of the stupid stigma of taking such meds. I should have done it back then because now I realize that having the right support and tools in place makes all the difference.

There has to be a point where we let all the second guessing and worry about what whoever may think go and just do what we need to do. You're just doing what you need to do to take care of yourself. It's really not that deep. I mean, really, who cares what anyone thinks. If someone has enough time to judge what I am doing in my life, then it seems to me that they may need to find a new hobby. I am not THAT interesting.

Playfulness and Curiosity

If you haven't noticed yet, We don't like to take life too seriously. Life's too short to take too seriously. Plus life is way more vibrant and fulfilling this way. Try it. Reconnect with your childhood sense of wonder and playfulness—it's fun. We don't care how old you are, Bopen to playfulness and curiosity. It really helps with creativity, adaptability, building resilience, and realizing your universal signs.

Embrace spontaneity and explore your surroundings with a sense of joy, wonder, and curiosity. Allow yourself to be silly, to belly laugh with your best friend in the middle of a crowded restaurant, and don't allow yourself to always act like a fuddy duddy grown up. Believe us, this can be a powerful antidote to some stress and pressures of daily fuddy duddy grown up life. Haven't you noticed how children always seem to take in everything with curiosity and wonder? They have no qualms one way or another about what's coming up. They don't fight with the natural way life unfolds. Bopen to the unexpected, there is no need to fight against the natural flow of life.

By being playful and curious, you will rediscover that same sense of wonder and openness to receive the signs given to you from the universe. Which leads me to my next Bopen requirement, having no expectations.

No Expectations

Expect nothing. We know, What? Have they lost their mind, again? How is that possible? Hear us out. Expectations create a sense of order or predictability, but if you pay attention, they often lead to disappointment and frustration when reality doesn't align with your visions. You don't need that stress. You never know how or when your signs will come, and you don't need to know, also don't be afraid to ask for a sign. Have faith that they will show up and they will be exactly what you need. It's about releasing the tight grip we often have on our preconceived notions of how things should be. Experience the world as it truly is. Remember, the universe hears you and will deliver. It will deliver on its time because that's what it does. You don't get to choose when your signs come or where. They may not come right away. It could be next week or the week after, but believe it will come.

Nurture flexibility in your thoughts and actions. It's not an easy ask, we know. Uncertainty is uncomfortable. It takes practice. You will learn to roll with the tides. I promise once you begin to start to feel comfortable with saying "I've done my part now let's see what happens," you will hold a new freedom handling change, and we know change is one thing that never changes.

Paying Attention

Sometimes, we're too busy to pay attention. We might be busy overthinking, or busy doing all the tasks that make up our lives. When we make ourselves too busy to pay attention the universe will get louder, and louder until you finally make the change. You know how some people seem to like to learn the hard way. They're simply not paying attention to their signs so the universe keeps hammering them with the same signs disguised differently until they finally realize something needs to change. Most likely they say, man I should have done that a long time ago. They could feel something inside, they just weren't allowing themself to Bopen to what it meant.

Chrissy

On the day I finally decided to commit to starting this book, the universe decided to unleash a series of several signs during my brief twelve-minute commute to our jewelry store. Six months had passed since I first met with Maria, a potential ghostwriter and writing coach, and it had been three weeks since our second meeting. Throughout this time, every attempt to abandon the project seemed to be met with a renewed urge to continue.

Seeking a final escape, I called my accountant while driving, hoping he might offer a practical reason to quit. Instead, he offered no discouragement. As we spoke, a pattern seemed to emerge: I passed not one, but several cars bearing license plates with the number 88. At a stoplight, a vivid red cardinal darted in front of my windshield, and as I parked, the phone rang with news that a dear friend and hair stylist, who had always lived by the mantra "no regrets," had passed away.

These signs seemed too important to ignore. I shifted my car into park, looked up at the jewelry store, and drafted an email to move the book project forward. I pressed send and stepped out of my car with a newfound determination. It was as if the universe itself was affirming my decision, pushing me towards a dream I'd nearly given up on. With each step towards the store, I felt a growing confidence in the journey ahead, inspired by memories and moments that felt guided by something greater than coincidence.

Taking Action

It would have been so easy for us to quit on this book and sink back into our boring comfort zone living full of regret telling us we should have done it. We didn't do that because we were Bbrave enough to make the move when a sign or in Chrissy's case many signs show up. You have to embrace the unknown and move forward even when the path ahead isn't clear. Be ready to take action when the universe nudges you.

It takes a bunch of courage to take action when you are unsure about what's coming next, but the courage to take a leap of faith can lead to remarkable outcomes. We took the leap and went forward with this book and look, now we're on Chapter 4. We think that's pretty cool! Think about a time when you followed a gut feeling and it led to something positive. Those moments stand out, right? Because it required you to Bbrave and trust in something bigger than you could understand, you trusted yourself, your instincts, and you accepted life's natural flow.

When you get a sign, it's an invitation to jump into Bfearless. As I said before, it's not about being without fear. Acknowledge your fear, feel your fear, and do the thing anyway. Trust that the universe is guiding you in the right direction, even if you envision a scary, dark path in a forest filled with grizzly bears. Take the risks because it's almost always worth it and the grizzly bears turn out to be cuddly, sweet, playful puppies.

Taking action when a sign comes is about embracing the opportunities that the universe presents. However, sometimes we may need to be a bit more proactive in seeking guidance. You need to learn to ask for signs.

Learn to Ask for Signs

Chrissy

When you put awareness and energy into it, you can learn to ask for your signs. A while back, I was making some changes at work, and, true to my nature, I found ourselves overthinking them (I know, shocker!). During this time, I was also reading the book *Signs: The Secret Language of the Universe* by Laura Lynne Jackson.[1]

In the book, Jackson declares that you can ask the universe for a specific, random sign to help you gain clarity. Intrigued, I decided to play with Jackson's concept a bit and asked for a sign that was very specific and random. I don't remember exactly how I phrased it, but it was something to do with the Spice Girls (I didn't even really remember liking them, I was more into David Beckham).

What a surprise when I got two signs in the same week. I was starting a yoga workout on my Peloton app when a Spice-Girls

---

[1]   Jackson, Laura L. 2018. *Signs: The Secret Language of the Universe.* New York: Dial Press Trade.

yoga workout popped up. Then, at work later that week, my mom waltzed into the jewelry store with a pile of People magazines to drop off, and the top one was a cover story about Victoria and David Beckham and their chickens. Wow! It worked!

Learning to ask for signs is pretty easy. There aren't any strict rules to follow or anything. You can ask away any time you want, but I find it works best for me to ask when I am naturally moving slow and quiet (like when I'm putting on my jewelry with the difficult clasps).

I don't care if it's on your way to work, taking a minute while you're getting dressed, or waiting for your coffee to brew, these are all perfect opportunities for you to have a little conversation with the universe.

Ask specific questions like, "I'm struggling a little today, am I supposed to have this second baby? Am I gonna be a mom some-day? Am I doing the right thing at my job? Should I hire this person? Should I marry this guy? Am I going to meet someone I actually want to marry? Can I really run a marathon? Should I sign up for the race? Can I really change my career at this point?

Sometimes we ask for specific signs without being aware that we are. In Jackson's book she had a story about a family griev-ing from the recent loss of their beloved wife/mother. One of the daughters while on vacation kept seeing piles of playing cards on a hike she and her husband were on. For whatever reason, the cards made her think of her mom, thinking if her mom was a card in a deck she would be the queen of hearts. She saw several decks of cards in random places on that hike. Weird, right? Her curiosity peaked after the third random deck of cards so she decided to investigate closer. When she walked up to those cards, they were all scattered face down, except for one card sitting off to the side by itself. You will never guess what card that was. Yep. It was the queen of hearts and it was face up. She knew that had to be her mom letting her know she was okay and she was still with her even from the other side. Even after vacation was over and she was back home, she started seeing the queen of hearts everywhere, in the most random places. She saw it in the form of tattoos on strangers, a queen of hearts playing card sewed into a curtain at a performance she was at, and even randomly hearing about a dress shop called The Queen of Hearts. Without really realizing it, she chose the queen of hearts as her sign and that hike was the quiet place that helped her open her awareness, mind, and heart to the possibility.

It's in these quiet moments you invite the universe to respond and guide you. Be honest with yourself about what you need clarity on and Bopen to the signs as they come your way. This is how you align yourself with the magical possibilities and guidance from the universe.

What You Can Do

We've explored Bopen—the practice of being open to the signs and possibilities the universe has to offer us. We talked about how being open to the unexpected can guide us to our true paths. We've learned the importance of starting before you are ready and you need to slow down and be quiet to recognize signs, we need to embrace childlike playfulness and curiosity. Life is unpredictable no matter how we plan it, we don't control the timeline of the universe.

Consider practicing Bopen in your life. Here are some ways that may help you get started on your way to Bopen:

Reflection Exercises: Spend a few moments each day quietly reflecting. Use this time to ask yourself specific questions, like what you are struggling with or guidance through a hard decision.

Write down any signs you notice throughout the day and reflect on their meaning.

Create Your Own Sign: Choose a specific sign you want to receive from the universe. Be very clear about what you want. Then all you have to do is remain open to when and where the sign appears.

Playfulness Challenge: Do activities you remember loving as a kid or try something completely new. Start painting or dancing or singing at the top of your lungs. The goal is to reconnect with a sense of wonder and curiosity.

By practicing Bopen, you invite the universe's guidance and embrace a journey filled with purpose, joy, and fulfillment. Remember the universe is always sending you signs—you just have to Bopen to receiving them. So, crawl, step, run out of your comfort zone, embrace the unknown, and see where your journey takes you.

RemindHer: Welcome new possibilities and experiences with an open heart and mind.

CHAPTER 7:

Bhealthy

Rae

Having a mindset and conscious awareness of what makes you feel like your best you is incredibly important. I'm not a health coach or nutritionist, but I do have an insane infatuation with meal prep, healthy eating, and teaching my kids about their food.

Of course, there are days where I don't get to eat the way I'd like to, but I know that starting my day with a vitamin rich green superfood powder and grabbing a protein bar for an on the go meal will give me the nutrition I need to sustain until I can make a healthy meal for myself. It's honestly a bit of pain to constantly doing meal prep for breakfasts, lunches and dinners but controlling the food you eat gives a guaranteed outcome—you know how you'll feel when you eat it. Personally, I like a guaranteed outcome so even when I may not want to make dinner, I make it anyway because I know the outcome is going to cost me less, my kids will actually eat it, and we will feel great after.

Another healthy habit I've made is working out. At least six days a week, I'll exercise. Even if I don't work out, I do something to get my endorphins going such as stretching, cold plunge, walking or drinking tea. And yes, all of this takes time. I'll get up before everyone else, set my coffee to brew the night before but the routines are all necessary for the guaranteed outcome. Setting up these routines will encourage health and give that guaranteed outcome. Even when we were on a family trip to Disney, I still got up to work out every morning for me. Granted, not everyone understood the 5am wake up but it's for my mental self along with my physical self. If I want to be my best self, my best mom and my best wife, I need to work out in the morning. This is how I start my day feeling joyful, energetic and alive.

Chrissy

I used to use deprivation dieting as a way to try to control my body. I'd get on the scale every morning and, if the number was lower than the day before I had a good day. If the number was higher, I started off the day planning to restrict calorie intake so I could assure a reduction the following morning. I was terrified that if I didn't do this, that if I slipped up a little bit, my body would get bigger in ways I didn't want, and I wouldn't be as worthy of love, belonging, and joy.

But, I've spent the last few chapters telling you that you deserve joy now, today. You deserve joy if you're in a skinny body or a larger one. You deserve joy if your stomach has stretch marks, and even if your thighs have some as well. You deserve joy in the body you have today, and the body you will have in the future.

Does this mean you need to eliminate all your body insecurities? No, I'm not even sure that's possible. I recently got dressed for an event and let Scarlet, who is twelve, pick my outfit. She picked a bright pink romper, heels, and a stack of bracelets. I slid into the romper and the first thing I noticed was the way the hem hit my thigh. Immediately my brain tried to tell me my thighs were too big, I should wear something else, I should disguise this part of me instead of drawing attention to it.

No, we can't eliminate insecurities. But, we can challenge them. Are my thighs too big or are they the powerful legs of a mother who is strong enough to carry her children and a woman who can run a marathon? I looked at my daughter who is trying to figure out how to be a woman in this world. Then, I brushed my hair and left the bedroom, and the mirror. I'd wear the shorts, I'd pose for the photos, and my thighs would stand out, proud, and strong.

A strong body leads to a strong mind and a strong life. Bstrong is about health as the foundation for everything. When you develop the discipline and knowledge to take care of your health, you are living the Bstrong life, which affects your mindset, your relationships, your energy levels, your outlook, and everything you want your life to be.

So, let's explore how to live a Bstrong life. We'll look at common obstacles, health strategies, and dealing with disease and injury. Health is a wide-ranging topic, but it comes back to one foundation. Your health is the key to your Bstrong life.

Health Is Not a Trend

We grew up in the fat-free movement, which shaped dietary habits and perceptions of health and nutrition. The notion that fat was the enemy dominated popular culture and influenced food manufacturing, marketing, and consumption patterns. From grocery store shelves lined with "low-fat" and "fat-free" products to public health campaigns advocating for reduced fat intake, it was an era of widespread fear of fat.

As time passed and research advanced, the narrative began to shift. While excessive consumption of certain types of fats, particularly trans fats and saturated fats, has been linked to health risks, it became evident that not all fats were created equal. Essential fatty acids play crucial roles in bodily functions.

Thinking about the time when everyone was crazy about fat-free foods makes us think hard about trends in food and health industries. It shows how much the media can sway our opinions. As we look at health and how it affects our lives, we will not jump on any trends. Bstrong is not about fads. We need solid, reasonable, and sustainable habits to build good health. We want to look at real-life problems and explore real-life solutions and health strategies.

Jennifer Moore is a women's health coach and trained health food chef. We brought her in for some expert guidance on health from someone who lives and works with women like us every day. "Women often come to me running on fumes. They're in this place where they're just surviving every day and barely have enough energy to care for themselves in the most basic ways," Moore said. She offers coaching programs designed to help women live their Bhealthy lives. Moore shared that, oftentimes, Bhealthy starts with ensuring you're satisfied in your career, your relationships, and the amount of joy in your life. If we aren't happy in these areas we tend to overcompensate with food and don't make time to exercise. Fortunately, though, she sees women make tiny shifts for their health that result in leveling up in other areas of their lives as well.

Common Complaints

Moore recommends a holistic approach to wellness to her clients. It's not just about what you eat and how you move your body. Rest, relaxation, and finding ways to care for your spirit matter too. "When we sit down to eat and we aren't present, or we're in fight, flight, or freeze our digestion doesn't work well because you don't need to eat when a bear is chasing you. Our bodies aren't programmed to eat and digest properly in a stressed-out state and this can lead to digestive issues."

It's easy to get psyched up to get in shape and develop a healthy lifestyle, but soon, there are some bumps in that road. Common complaints surrounding health often reflect underlying issues that may come from many areas of life. Let's explore some of these complaints:

Feeling tired: Fatigue can result from a variety of reasons, such as poor sleep quality, insufficient physical activity, high stress levels, or underlying medical conditions like anemia or thyroid disorders.

Solutions include:

Addressing sleep hygiene.

Managing stress.

Maintaining a balanced diet.

Incorporating regular exercise.

Clothes not fitting comfortably: Weight gain or changes in body composition can make clothes feel tighter or less comfortable. This could be attributed to overeating, hormonal imbalances, or psychological factors such as emotional eating or body image issues. It's important to remember that simply increasing physical activity isn't always the solution. Sometimes, it's about changing your routine to better align with your goals. For example, if you have been focused on cardio for years without seeing the desired results, consider adding resistance training to your regimen. Different types of activities can lead to different outcomes, so it might be time to explore new ways to move your body.

Solutions include:

Adopting healthier eating habits.

Adjusting your exercise routine to incorporate a mix of cardio and strength training.

Seeking support from a healthcare professional or nutritionist.

Feeling "icky": This vague sensation of discomfort could indicate various issues, including digestive problems, food intolerances, dehydration, or even emotional distress.

Solutions include:

Keeping track of dietary triggers.

Staying hydrated.

Practicing mindful eating.

Seeking medical advice if symptoms persist.

Persistent bloating: Bloating can be caused by several factors, including gas accumulation, overeating, food intolerances, or gastrointestinal issues like irritable bowel syndrome (IBS).

Solutions include:

Keeping a food diary.

Identifying trigger foods.

Practicing portion control.

Incorporating gut-friendly foods and fiber-rich foods.

Consulting with a healthcare provider may be necessary to rule out underlying digestive issues.

The discrepancy between blood work results and how you feel: Standard blood work results may not always reflect how an individual feels on a day-to-day basis. While blood tests provide valuable information about overall health and specific biomarkers, they may not capture subjective feelings of fatigue, discomfort, or malaise.

Solutions include communicating openly with healthcare providers about symptoms and concerns, as additional testing or adjustments to treatment plans may be necessary to address underlying issues and improve overall well-being.

There is no shortage of complaints, but there are also an equal number of solutions if you're willing to look for them. Bstrong means never giving in to complaints and excuses. Find solutions, build strategies, and build the healthy life you want.

Does this list of solutions feel overwhelming? We're not going to tell you they are easy, but we can tell you that continuing to feel "off" is hard too. This book is about micro shifts to move yourself toward the life you want. So, pick one thing. Get bloodwork done, eat more veggies this week than you did last week, take a ten-minute walk each day this week (or two days!).

Bhealthy Strategies

Bstrong doesn't just happen. It comes from knowledge, strategy, and the effort that makes it happen. I want to give you some real-life strategies you can use to make a difference. These are not trendy ideas or quick fixes. These are realistic, tried-and-true methods to build a healthy life. It's not about shortcuts. It's results that last.

Slay the Scale

Chrissy

A critical decision for me was to toss my scale. It was more than a rebellious act against a piece of bathroom furniture. It was a liberation from the mental shackles that had me imprisoned in a cycle of self-deprivation and obsessive dieting. For too long, I allowed that simple number on the scale to dictate how I felt about myself each day.

It wasn't just me caught in this vicious cycle. My husband also found himself ensnared in the same trap. Together, we set deadlines for shedding pounds, viewing weight loss as a race against time rather than a journey toward health and vitality.

The decision to rid our home of the scale scared me at first. I wondered if I would lose control and spiral into unhealthy habits without this daily check-in. Doubt consumed me.

Yet, things slowly began to change. A newfound sense of freedom started to come over me. I learned to redirect my focus toward building strength and nourishing my body with wholesome foods. Strength training transformed my perspective. I am no longer fixated on a number each morning. Instead, I celebrated the tangible progress of my physical capabilities. I can lift more this week than I did last week, I can see my shoulder muscles developing, and my quads make that bright pink romper Scarlet loves even more attractive. I've developed a stronger physique and a healthier mindset. That number on a scale has been replaced with values like self-care and self-love.

Give Up Perfection

Do you feel like you have to be perfect in everything you do to be healthy? Many of us get caught up in meeting excessive standards with our diets, exercise routines, appearance, and productivity, and the media doesn't help. Jennifer Moore shared that it's really about what we do most of the time that matters and that we shouldn't skip birthday treats and an occasional dinner out to celebrate life. In order to stick with something long term you need to make it flexible enough for a girl's night out.

Moore also shared that it's important to think about the lengths you're willing to go to accomplish your health goals. Some women want to have visible abs until they realize that a diet of baked chicken, brown rice, and broccoli is really difficult to stick to. If your weekly treat, wine night, or indulgent meal is important to you, that's great. Enjoy it, and worry less about abs.

Research has shown that "In the U.S., females are exposed to messages about how they should look from the moment they are born. Teens and young girls are also more likely to be given praise for how they look rather than for their actions or thoughts.

"They are also constantly shown images through the media of unrealistic standards. Many of the images have been altered using technology, causing these young females to strive for body ideals and beauty that do not actually exist."[2]

This can lead to an array of mental health problems including:
- Low self-esteem
- Eating disorders
- Depression
- Anxiety
- Social isolation

Being healthy isn't about being perfect. It's about being consistent and finding balance. It's not about always following strict rules or feeling guilty when we treat ourselves now and then. Instead, it's about making choices that we can stick with and that make us feel good in the long run.

To accomplish this, you might consider the 80/20 Rule. "The 80/20 rule typically refers to eating nutritious foods 80 percent

2   rench, Mandy. "What Is the Connection between Beauty Standards and Mental Health?" MedicalNewsToday. May 1, 2024. https://www.medicalnewstoday.com/articles/beauty-standards-and-mental-health#mental-health-conditions.

of the time, then eating more freely the other 20 percent of the time. Unlike a restrictive diet plan, the 80/20 rule focuses on moderation . . ."[3]

The great thing about this plan is that it allows us to focus on our health without perfectionism. Nobody's perfect. We are going to have moments of indulgence, and these do not need to be seen as failure. If we set the bar to an unrealistic level, we are more likely to quit when we can't reach it. A healthy dose of moderation can leave perfectionism behind and embrace a realistic life of health and well-being.

Instead of aiming for perfection, let's focus on making progress. Let's celebrate the little wins—like eating a healthy meal, finishing a workout, or taking time for self-care—knowing that each step gets us closer to our goals.

Get Moving

Something is always better than nothing. Whether it's squeezing in a short workout or taking a brisk five-minute walk, every bit of movement counts towards improving our overall health and well-being. The key is to find what truly ignites our passion for movement—whether it's dancing, hiking, swimming, or cycling—and make it a regular part of our lives.

Not only does regular exercise benefit our physical health by strengthening our heart and muscles, but it also plays a crucial role in supporting our mental well-being. Movement can release endorphins, reduce stress, and lower cortisol levels—the hormone associated with stress response.

---

3   Bradley, Sarah and Andi Breitowich. "What Is The 80/20 Rule Diet? Pros, Cons, And Healthy Foods To Eat, According To MDs." Women's Health. July 2, 2024. https://www.medicalnewstoday.com/articles/beauty-standards-and-mental-health#mental-health-conditions.

Chrissy

However, it's essential to approach exercise with mindfulness and self-awareness. As I'm discovering during my journey through perimenopause, pushing myself to the limit with intense exercise like marathon running didn't yield the expected results. Instead of achieving the flat stomach and weight loss I anticipated, I found myself facing unexpected bloating and increased inflammation. Yep, running a ton made me bigger, but it had so many benefits for my mental and physical health as well as my relationships, that I don't regret it. It's just funny that Danny and I started training to lose weight and I experienced the opposite.

It wasn't until later that I realized the toll that excessive exercise took on my body. The physical stress of marathon training triggered a surge in cortisol levels, contributing to inflammation and sabotaging my efforts to achieve my desired physique.

This experience taught me a valuable lesson: Spirit care matters as much as physical activity. If an exercise regimen feels like a chore or doesn't align with our true passions, we're less likely to stick with it in the long run. Instead, we should listen to our inner voice and seek out movement that brings us joy. The key to sustainable fitness lies in finding the balance between pushing ourselves to grow and honoring our body's need for rest and rejuvenation.

Muscle Up

Chrissy

I know I've talked about my thighs a lot, but I'm going to mention them and the romper again. When I put that romper on I'd been working for a while on strength training which challenged my long-held beliefs about the need to weigh less. Muscle makes me weigh more, but, since I'm not jumping on the scale anymore it doesn't matter. Muscle makes me tighter /toned/ more fit because it takes up less space even though it weighs more.

When you think of muscle building, you might picture heavy weights and intense gym workouts. Yet, adding some strength exercises to your daily routine can be pretty easy and convenient. Even simple things, like doing pushups against the kitchen counter or working in some squats while doing household chores, can help you get stronger and keep your muscles in good shape.

Some people think that strength training will make women look too bulky or muscular. That's simply not true. Women don't have as much of the hormone testosterone as men, which is what makes muscles big. So, doing strength exercises will give you a more toned and fit look, along with lots of health benefits.

That's why it's a good idea for women of any age to include strength training in their exercise routine, but particularly as we age. Research has shown that a big culprit for losing our physical abilities as we grow older is the age-related loss of muscle mass and strength, which is called sarcopenia. Typically, muscle mass and strength increase steadily from birth and reach their peak at around thirty to thirty-five years of age. After that, muscle power and performance decline slowly and linearly at first, and then faster after age sixty-five for women and seventy for men.[4]

Building muscle helps women keep their bodies healthy, stay independent as they get older, and have a better quality of life.

---

4   National Institute on Aging. "How Can Strength Training Build Healthier Bodies as We Age?" National Institute on Aging, September 14, 2023. https://www.nia.nih.gov/news/how-can-strength-training-build-healthier-bodies-we-age.

Nourishment

"So many women I work with grew up in the diet culture craze and are afraid to eat more than a certain number of low calories a day. If that's all they're eating, they're missing out on essential nutrition," Moore said in our interview. She went on to explain that women often under-eat protein and are afraid of carbohydrates or fat, fearing weight gain. But food isn't the enemy, it's fuel. While Moore encourages her clients to aim for around one hundred grams of protein a day, she emphasizes that this isn't enough on its own. As women age, they naturally lose muscle mass, so strength training is crucial alongside a balanced diet. It's about nourishing your body with the right foods and supporting it with the right kind of exercise.

Choosing nourishing foods means choosing foods that are good for your overall health and wellness instead of ones that just taste good. Nourishing foods are the ones that are packed with nutrients. These foods keep our bodies running well and help our minds stay sharp. Here are some important things to think about when you're choosing nourishing foods over comfort food:

- **Nutrient Density:** Nourishing foods give us energy, help keep our immune systems strong, and help our bodies heal. Things like fresh fruits and veggies, whole grains, lean meats, and good fats are full of nutrients.
- **Long-Term Health:** While comfort foods might make us feel good for a short time, eating them too much can lead to problems like gaining weight, inflammation, and problems like heart disease and diabetes. Choosing nourishing foods helps us stay healthy in the long run.
- **Balanced Eating:** Nourishing foods give us a bit of everything our bodies need. Eating mostly whole foods and staying away from processed foods helps keep our blood

sugar steady, makes our digestion better, and helps us manage our weight.

- **Mindful Eating:** Eating nourishing foods encourages us to pay attention to when we're hungry or full, enjoy the taste and texture of our food, and think about how food makes us feel physically and emotionally. This helps us have a healthier relationship with food and make choices that are good for us.

- **Emotional Well-Being:** While comfort foods might give us a temporary boost when we're stressed or sad, nourishing foods can also boost our mood and help us handle stress better. Some nutrients and certain vitamins in these foods are linked to feeling happier and thinking more clearly.

It's okay to enjoy comfort foods once in a while as part of a balanced diet (our families certainly enjoy an ice cream run and a pasta night) but focusing on nourishing foods most of the time can make you healthier physically and mentally, building your Bstrong life.

Drink Water

Water is often called the "elixir of life," and it is for good reason. Giving our bodies the water we need is one of the most critical things we can do, but many people don't realize how important it is. Think about this: we can go a few weeks without food, but we can only last a few days without water. That one simple example to show how crucial water is for us to stay alive.

Here are just a few of the benefits water gives us:

- Every cell, tissue, and organ needs water to work properly.
- Water helps keep our body temperature right.
- Water helps us digest food.

- Water helps our bodies use nutrients.
- We have more energy.
- Our brains work better.
- Our skin looks healthier.
- Our muscles and joints stay healthy.
- Water boosts our immune system.
- Water helps our bodies get rid of waste and toxins.
- Water carries nutrients and oxygen to our cells.
- Water helps keep our electrolytes balanced.

"The U.S. National Academies of Sciences, Engineering, and Medicine determined that an adequate daily fluid intake is:
- About 15.5 cups (3.7 liters) of fluids a day for men.
- About 11.5 cups (2.7 liters) of fluids a day for women.

You might need to modify your total fluid intake based on several factors:
- **Exercise.** If you do any activity that makes you sweat, you need to drink extra water to cover the fluid loss. It's important to drink water before, during and after a workout.
- **Environment.** Hot or humid weather can make you sweat and requires additional fluid. Dehydration also can occur at high altitudes.
- **Overall Health.** Your body loses fluids when you have a fever, vomiting or diarrhea. Drink more water or follow a doctor's recommendation to drink oral rehydration solutions. Other conditions that might require increased fluid intake include bladder infections and urinary tract stones.

- **Pregnancy and Breastfeeding.** If you are pregnant or breastfeeding, you may need additional fluids to stay hydrated."[5]

Think through Caffeine and Alcohol

Are you feeling tired lately? It might be because you've been drinking too much caffeine or alcohol. Research shows that "Caffeine may produce detrimental effects on subsequent sleep, resulting in daytime sleepiness."[6]

Try cutting back on how much caffeine you have, especially before bedtime. It could be the solution to your sleep and energy issues.

Alcohol can also mess with our sleep and make us feel tired. Even though it might make us feel relaxed at first, it can make sleep less restful. This leaves us feeling groggy in the morning.

Studies have shown that "Alcohol is traditionally known to have a relaxing effect. However, persons who consume alcohol in excessive amounts suffer from poor sleep quality and patients with alcohol use disorders commonly report insomnia."[7]

To see how caffeine and alcohol affect your energy, try keeping track of how much you have and how you feel in the morning. Write down when and how much coffee or alcohol you have each day and how you feel when you wake up.

---

5   "How Much Water Do You Need?" MayoClinic.Com. The Mayo Clinic, July 2, 2024. https://www.mayoclinic.org/healthy-lifestyle/nutrition-and-healthy-eating/in-depth/water/art-20044256.

6   Snell, Jan, and Monicque M. Lorist. "Progress in Brain Research: Chapter 6—Effects of Caffeine on Sleep and Cognition." *Science Direct* 190, (2011): 105–117. Accessed September 27, 2024. https://doi.org/10.1016/B978-0-444-53817-8.00006-2.

7   Park, S. Y., Oh, M. K., Lee, B. S., et. al. "The Effects of Alcohol on Quality of Sleep." *Korean Journal of Family Medicine,* 36(6), (2015): 294–299. Accessed September 27, 2024. https://doi.org/10.4082/kjfm.2015.36.6.294.

This simple process can help you decide if you need to cut back. Less caffeine and alcohol, especially in the evening, might help you sleep better and feel more awake during the day.

Don't Be Hungry

We don't like being hungry. We bet you don't either. It's uncomfortable, and if you ignore it long enough, you'll wind up with a headache. Put off eating a bit longer, and you'll tip into hangry territory, which isn't good for you or for your relationships. Besides, eating is joyful, and we're all about joy here. You don't have to feel hungry all the time or give up things you enjoy to have a healthy diet.

We've tried lots of diets, so we know how frustrating and unsatisfying it can be to follow strict eating plans. Feeling hungry all the time and craving certain foods can make it hard to stick to any diet for long.

Here is some great news: You don't have to feel hungry to be healthy. Choosing healthy meals and snacks with loads of protein can keep your body fueled and stave off hunger. By taking a more balanced and flexible approach to eating, you can give your body what it needs while still enjoying the foods you like.

You can even have dessert! You can include a reasonable portion of dessert in your routine. Pick desserts that have good ingredients and taste great. You can satisfy your sweet tooth without ruining your progress.

Moore shared some final words with us, and we think there couldn't be a better way to end this chapter. "I don't want you to think about less. Don't say I want to be smaller, I need to eat less, I need to watch less television. Thinking about restrictions doesn't work. Instead, think about more. You want more energy, more water, more protein, more weight lifting, more steps in your day, more nutrient-dense food, and more satiety. You want more joy." If you want to connect with Jennifer and learn more about her health programs find her on social media using @jmoorehealth.

RemindHer: Commit to taking care of your body, mind, and spirit so you can live your most vibrant life.

CHAPTER 8

Bstrong

My bracelet reminds me of the fact no matter what life brings you to just keep being strong and continue carrying on for the best outcome. The universe has a funny way of throwing tough situations at you but it's how we handle them that makes us who we are. I got my first B Strong bracelet after leaving an abusive relationship. My second B strong bracelet I got during one of the hardest times in my life. I am a graduate student studying to get my Nurse Practitioner, I'm in clinical and working full time. We recently received the health news no one ever wants to hear about a member of my family. We have two options each day and I choose to wake up and Bstrong. To get through our days and it will all workout! To Bstrong means to keep moving forward, manifesting positive outcomes. Life can be challenging but rallying together and being strong makes a positive difference.

~MARISSA LAMB

Melissa, a mother of five boys, had just been diagnosed with metastatic breast cancer. The youngest of her children was only three years old. She came into our jewelry store one day and shared her health update with our brother, Lewis. They were close—their sons were practically inseparable. The weight of her words hung in the air, a stark contrast to the vibrant energy that usually fills the store.

This was the same day our first sample of the Power to B bracelets arrived—a collection designed to inspire and empower. We didn't hesitate. Lewis picked up the Bstrong bracelet, a simple yet powerful reminder of resilience, and placed it on Melissa's wrist. "You need this," he said, passing on a secret weapon for the battle ahead.

Melissa never took that bracelet off. For the next eight years, she fought an uphill battle against an incurable disease. Every day was a new challenge, a new piece of news that could have easily broken anyone's spirit. But not Melissa. She knew that cancer would eventually take her life, but she refused to let it take her days. She lived each one to its fullest, creating beautiful memories for her boys, engaging fully with life, and touching the hearts of everyone around her.

The strength in Melissa's spirit is something we'll always remember. She embodied what it means to be Bstrong. If you're wearing that bracelet, or if you choose it as your power word for the day, you're channeling the same resilience that Melissa showed us all. She taught us that even in the face of the most daunting challenges, you can stand tall, breathe deeply, and carry on with grace and courage.

So many women in our community and beyond, despite focusing on health and well-being, wind up navigating major setbacks. Cancer, autoimmune diseases, major injuries—these are not uncommon, but that doesn't make them any easier to deal with. The truth is, we can't always control what happens to us. Life can be unpredictable, throwing curveballs that can shake us to our core. But what we can control is how we respond to these challenges. And that's where the concept of Bstrong comes in.

Bstrong isn't about always putting forward a strong, socially acceptable front. It's about acknowledging that stress, anxiety, depression, sadness, and loneliness are normal parts of life. It's about recognizing that these emotions don't make us weak; they make us human. When we acknowledge them instead of suppressing them, we strip away their power. We don't have to be controlled by our emotions, even when they're difficult to handle.

To be Bstrong is to stand firm on your own two feet, hands on your hips in a superwoman pose, knowing that whatever you're going through, it will pass. It's about taking a deep breath and, in that exhale, releasing the sense of panic that tries to take hold. It's about trusting that this moment of discomfort, no matter how intense, is temporary. When you embrace Bstrong, you remind yourself that even though this current struggle feels overwhelming, you have the inner strength to get through it. You will power your way through this because what lies on the other side of the struggle is meant for you.

Embracing Bstrong starts with the simple yet powerful act of acknowledging your emotions. We live in a society that often tells us to suppress our feelings, to "stay strong" and not let anyone see us sweat. But the truth is, suppressing emotions only gives them more power. When we pretend that everything is okay when it's not, we deny ourselves the opportunity to heal and grow.

Emotions are like waves—they rise, peak, and eventually recede. What keeps emotions lingering is our tendency to dwell on it, to ruminate and replay the thoughts that triggered it in the first place. But when we acknowledge our emotions without judgment, we allow them to pass through us more quickly. We can feel the fear, the sadness, or the anger, but we don't have to let it control us.

Take a moment to reflect on the last time you felt overwhelmed by an emotion. Did you try to push it away? Did you ignore it, hoping it would just disappear? Or did you sit with it, acknowledge it, and allow yourself to feel it fully? When we acknowledge our emotions, we can start to release them. We can say to ourselves, "Okay, brain, we're not letting this run away with our peace." It's a simple but powerful shift in perspective that allows us to regain control over our emotional state.

Sandy is another incredible woman who exemplifies what it means to be Bstrong. Living with advanced breast cancer, Sandy has faced numerous hardships and undergone countless treatments. Yet, every day, she wakes up and focuses on her health. Whether she's running, practicing yoga, or finding other ways to move her body, Sandy remains committed to staying active and strong. Her mental toughness is just as impressive as her physical resilience. She knows that every step she takes is a step toward living fully, despite the challenges she faces.

Bstrong isn't just about physical strength. It's about mental resilience, the ability to bounce back from tough times, and the determination to face problems head-on. They remind us that what we do and how we think can make all the difference when we're going through hard times.

Bstrong: Cultivate Mental Resilience

Building mental resilience is crucial to embracing the Bstrong mindset. It's about developing the ability to recover from setbacks, adapt to change, and keep going in the face of adversity. The good news is that resilience isn't something you're born with; it's something you can cultivate over time.

Daily habits play a significant role in building resilience. Physical activity, for example, is a powerful way to strengthen not just your body but also your mind. Exercise releases endorphins, which are natural mood boosters, and helps reduce stress levels. Mindfulness practices, such as meditation or deep breathing, can also help you stay grounded and focused, even when life feels chaotic.

Positive self-talk is another essential tool for building resilience. The way you speak to yourself has a profound impact on how you handle challenges. When you practice self-compassion and remind yourself of your inner strength, you're more likely to stay calm and composed in the face of adversity.

Emotional regulation is a key aspect of resilience. Techniques like deep breathing, journaling, and cognitive reframing can help you manage your emotions more effectively. When you feel overwhelmed, try taking a few deep breaths to calm your nervous system. Write down your thoughts and feelings to gain clarity and perspective. And if you find yourself stuck in negative thinking, try reframing the situation in a more positive light.

The Role of Community and Support

No one is an island and having a strong support system is essential to embracing Bstrong. Whether it's friends, family, or a community of like-minded women, surrounding yourself with people who understand and support you can make all the difference.

Open conversations about mental health and emotional well-being are crucial. When we talk about our struggles, we normalize the experience of difficult emotions and create a safe space for others to do the same. This isn't about seeking sympathy; it's about setting an example and breaking the stigma around mental health.

Being part of a supportive community also means being there for others. When you share your experiences, you help others feel less alone. And when you offer support, you reinforce your own resilience.

Bstrong on the Good Days, the Hard Days, and Every Day Between

Bstrong isn't just something you tap into during major life crises; it's a mindset you can apply to everyday challenges. Whether you're dealing with a health problem, recovering from an injury, or simply going through a rough patch in life, the Bstrong mindset can help you navigate these challenges with grace and resilience.

Start by building habits that support your physical and mental well-being. Make time for regular exercise, even if it's just a short walk. Practice mindfulness to stay centered and focused. And remember to be kind to yourself—self-compassion is a powerful tool for maintaining your mental strength.

When you feel overwhelmed, take a moment to breathe. Stand tall, like a superwoman, and remind yourself that this too shall pass. You don't have to have all the answers right now; you just have to keep going, one step at a time.

> RemindHer: Build resilience and strength to face life's ups and downs with confidence.

CHAPTER 9

Bsexy

Chrissy

On the night of my wedding, I had pictured the perfect ending—a romantic and passionate conclusion to an already magical day. But after hours of celebrating, greeting guests, and dancing until our feet ached, Danny and I were completely drained. As we finally undressed and crawled into bed, any thoughts of passion evaporated. We were simply too exhausted.

Instead of the steamy night I had imagined, we fell asleep almost immediately, tangled in sheets, but not in each other. At the time, I felt a twinge of guilt, as if I had failed some unspoken marital rite. I kept the story to myself, thinking it was something to be ashamed of, something I shouldn't tell people about.

Here's what I know now: having sex on your wedding night can be great, but not having sex on your wedding night can also be a great decision. The truth is, sex—whether on your wedding night, or any other time—is always a choice. So many factors affect your libido and desire, and it's okay to sit it out when you need to. It's also okay to dive in with enthusiasm when the mood strikes.

As the years have passed, I've come to understand that there's no right or wrong way to approach your sex life, whether it's on your wedding night or any other night. What's important is that you honor where you are, physically and emotionally, without feeling pressured to meet some external expectation.

Rae

The hardest thing I've had to communicate in my relationship is to get my husband to understand that I'm not a water faucet; I can't just be turned on and off at a moment's notice. For me, feeling connected sexually requires more than just a single moment or a specific action. I need attention throughout the day, those little gestures that make me feel noticed and appreciated touches that are affectionate without expectation, words that make me feel seen.

It took time for me to learn this about myself, and even more time to learn how to communicate it effectively. But I realized that understanding how I'm wired and finding ways to express that are vital. There is power in words and power in communication, especially when it comes to something as intimate as sex.

Talking about sex can be tricky. You have to be brave enough to bring up the challenging conversations, to get comfortable with the uncomfortable. But that's how you grow. For me, being open about what I need has transformed not only my relationship but also how I see myself. My husband is happy to give me what I want, but he isn't a mind reader. I have to take the time to thoughtfully explain my needs clearly.

Dr. Stokes: Sexuality on Your Own Terms

Sexuality isn't a one-size-fits-all experience. To explore this further, we spoke with Dr. Michael Stokes, a licensed mental health counselor and sex therapist, who introduced me to the Autonomous Sexuality Model.

> *In the Autonomous Sexuality Model, you call the shots. You design what works for you rather than following some narrative of what society says you should do. It's about accepting where you are in life—whether you're single, married, with kids, or in any other stage. Sex may not always be the slow, passionate scene it once was. Sometimes, it might be quick, messy, and squeezed into the midst of multitasking.*
>
> *When life is busy—kids, work, all the demands you face—sexuality can become another task to manage. But it's important to remember that this phase of life, like all others, is temporary. Being flexible and adjusting to where you are now is key.*
>
> **~DR. STOKES**

Dr. Stokes emphasized the importance of defining your own sexuality, especially during times of change, such as after having children. Our own experiences align perfectly with this philosophy. We've come to understand that sexuality evolves, and what matters most is finding what works for you in the present moment. Our path to feeling sexy looks different now than it did when we were in our twenties, and when we were first married. And according to Dr. Stokes, it will morph again once our children are grown. Our job is to try to accept the changes and find ways to Bsexy in the phase of life we're in now. Dr. Stokes:

You always have the freedom to define your sexuality. The key is understanding your current reality. Kids, careers, and responsibilities will bring changes to your life, including your sex life. It's essential to cut out the noise of what society or your friends say your sex life should be like. Focus on what you desire, which will naturally change over time.

Embracing Flexibility and Open Communication

One of the most important takeaways from our conversation with Dr. Stokes is the importance of flexibility and open communication within relationships. Dr. Stokes:

It's crucial to express your desires without judgment. However, expressing those desires doesn't mean they can always be met. It's okay to say, 'I'd love to have sex multiple times a week, but I just don't have it in me right now.' Healthy communication involves sharing your thoughts and hearing your partner's desires, then finding a balance that works for both of you. It's also important to stay out of the headspace of wishing for something else. This is where you are right now in life, so focus on the connection you have, even if it's just a few minutes. Remember, ebbs and flows are normal because life happens.

Dr. Stokes's insights remind us that Bsexy isn't just about sex; it's about connecting with and understanding your own sexuality. It's about exploring your desires, communicating openly, and finding ways to feel good in your own skin.

Some women find their Bsexy energy when they're dressed in Bermuda shorts and ankle-deep in garden soil. For others, it might be a sundress and sandals. The trick is to find what works for you. To learn more from Dr. Stokes visit www.DrMichaelStokes.com.

Chrissy

On our wedding night, we sat in a Jacuzzi and talked about how much fun we had that day, and how happy we were to be married. The truth is that even though we didn't have sex on our wedding night, when I fell asleep I was in my Bsexy place. I was relaxed, joyful, and living as my favorite version of myself.

Now, after sixteen years of marriage I can tell you honestly that Bsexy is something you have to work at. In the early days of our marriage, before kids, we were free to enjoy sexy time together whenever we wanted. Then, when our kids were small it sometimes felt like lightyears passed without a moment to cuddle before passing out at night. Now, Danny and I sometimes fall into a pattern of work, home, dishes, laundry, and fling into bed at night. We have to consciously make a choice to include date nights and alone time in our calendar. It's so easy to deprioritize your need to Bsexy, but playfulness is vital to maintain joy in your life.

I have to work on remaining playful so I don't wind up feeling resentful about the dynamic that naturally exists in my marriage. I need and want physical affection more than my husband. I'm sharing this with you because I know that women often hear that men want sexual attention more and when you're the more high touch partner you can feel like maybe something is wrong with you. It's not. There is nothing wrong with being a woman who enjoys physical affection, needs physical affection, and asks for physical affection.

If I'm feeling playful, and Danny and I are in the kitchen together I can look for the opportunities for fun and connection. If Danny grabs me and kisses me, my kids scream about how gross it is, and suddenly we're laughing. If I let myself get in a resentful space because I want more affection than I'm getting, I bristle or back away and the air between us feels heavier. Now, maintaining this isn't just my responsibility, it's Danny's as well, but my responsibility is to let Danny know what I need, and to try to meet his needs where I can.

One of the ways I can work at this is to ensure I'm taking care of myself. I feel the sexiest when I'm relaxed and rested. Sometimes that's when I'm dressed for a date night and Danny tells me how beautiful I look. Other times, I feel light, free, and comfortable with my makeup-free face and simple clothing, or when I'm in bed with my husband, stripped down to the most vulnerable version of myself. In each of these moments, I'm relaxed, playful, silly, and confident.

Jewelry makes me feel sexy too—a simple outfit with a beautiful piece I love, the finishing touch that says, "I took a moment for myself today."

Rae

For me, Bsexy is about feeling good in my body, whether that's through the way I dress, the jewelry I wear, or the way I take care of myself. It's about being connected to myself, and that connection makes me feel empowered. Empowerment is sexy.

One of the ways I feel most attractive, both to myself and my partner, is when I'm showered, with my hair done and makeup on, but dressed in comfy yoga gear and nice jewelry. The jewelry elevates how I feel—it has meaning, sentiment, and it just gives me energy. It's not about putting on a show; it's about how I feel inside, and that's what connects me to my sexuality.

Redefining Sexuality on Your Terms

Sexuality is an ever-evolving aspect of life. It's influenced by countless factors—stress, hormones, relationships, and overall health. But at its core, it's about how you feel in your own skin. Being in touch with your sexuality is about being in touch with yourself, your desires, and your needs. It's about embracing the changes and challenges with flexibility and openness.

Dr. Stokes's Autonomous Sexuality Model empowers us to define our own sexual expression, free from societal expectations. It encourages us to communicate our desires openly, be flexible with our needs, and most importantly, be kind to ourselves as we navigate the ebbs and flows of life.

So whether you find your Bsexy in a sundress, yoga gear, or simply in your skin, know that it's your journey to define. Embrace your sexuality as a vital part of your overall well-being, and let it be a source of joy, connection, and empowerment in your life.

Your Right to Pleasure

Bsexy is not just about feeling attractive in the traditional sense; it's about reclaiming your right to seek pleasure and joy in every facet of your life. It's a mindset that encourages you to prioritize what makes you feel good, not just in your body, but in your heart and mind too. Yes, it can mean during sex, but Bsexy also encompasses all the little things that delight you.

Imagine the first scent and sip of that delicious organic French roast coffee you brewed at home. Or consider this: does your weekly calendar include more than one thing meant to make your day more pleasant or joyful? It should. Start by looking at your calendar or to-do list and ask yourself, "How can I make this thing more joyful, more pleasant, more pleasurable?" (And yes, "pleasurable" is absolutely a word.)

Because what we know for sure is that most women feel some degree of shame when they hear the word "pleasure." Society has conditioned us to associate pleasure with something that requires permission or that comes with conditions—like wearing uncomfortable thigh-high lacy something to Bsexy. But sexy can be redefined by each woman, in her own way, to simply mean that she feels sexy and is making time and finding ways to fit in more pleasure and joy in the things she already does.

Bsexy Is about Ease

Sexy is not about conforming to a specific look or fulfilling someone else's fantasy. It's about feeling at ease in your own skin, embracing what makes you feel alive, and allowing yourself the space to experience joy. It's the world we still live in—where dishes need to be done, but why not make that more pleasurable by turning on some music you can sing or move to? Or if lace lingerie makes you feel sexy but you don't think you'll actually wear it much, maybe buy yourself a new beautiful bra with lace accents and matching bottoms, and do it for YOU.

Remember, Bsexy is about you first. If someone else enjoys the Bsexy vibe you've got going on, that's great, but the focus is on what makes you feel good. Most likely, you can't even remember the last time you took your time to choose the perfect bra that is both beautiful and makes you feel sexy. And for God's sake, get rid of the ones you've had for three years or seventeen years—it's time for something new that makes you feel amazing.

Bridging Pleasure and Joy

It's time to bridge the gap between the word "pleasure" and the initial feeling of shame that the world has taught us to associate with it. Pleasure is just another form of joy, and you deserve it all. More pleasure in your Bsexy life means more joy for you. So, ask yourself: How can I make this task or experience I'm planning more lovely for myself? When we focus on bringing pleasure into our lives we are more likely to turn on music while we make dinner, or take a breath before diving into lunch at the office. Bsexy is about taking the time to lean into delight and give yourself the opportunity for pleasure.

When you redefine Bsexy, you reclaim the power to design a life where joy and pleasure are woven throughout your everyday experiences. It's about being unapologetically you, living with intention, and finding joy in the details of life.

Action Steps to Bsexy:

- **Joyful Rituals:** Identify a daily or weekly ritual that brings you pleasure and make it a non-negotiable part of your routine. This could be a bath, a walk in nature, reading a novel in the evening, self-love time, or anything else that brings you joy and pleasure.

- **Reframe Tasks:** Look at your to-do list and choose one task you can make more enjoyable—whether by adding music, a favorite drink, or simply shifting your mindset.

- **Treat Yourself:** Invest in something that makes you feel sexy and empowered—whether it's lingerie, a bottle of perfume, or a new piece of jewelry that brings you joy.

- **Release the Old:** Go through your wardrobe and let go of anything that no longer makes you feel amazing. Replace it with something that does.

Redefining sexy is an ongoing process of discovering what brings you joy and embracing it fully. Remember, Bsexy is about feeling good in your life and your skin, on your terms.

RemindHer: Embrace your unique beauty and confidence, radiate from the inside out.

CHAPTER 10

Bsupported

Chrissy

Our brother Lewis, Rae, and I aren't big huggers. On my wedding day, though, I remember the hug Lewis gave me. It was an "I'm happy for you and am so honored to be here" kind of hug. That may have been the last hug I got from him. But, one thing is certain, even when we disagree, even if he doesn't totally get me, he will support me at every turn. Lewis is our business partner, the uncle to our children, and so much more. I get to walk through the world with the comforting knowledge that I have a support system that will never abandon me. Thanks Lewis.

We recognize how lucky we are to have this support system—our family is always there. We know that for many of you, your family can't or won't be the support system you need. If that's the case, we want to encourage you to find your people and Bsupported during the hard days, the good days, and all the days in between.

Imagine waking up every day feeling full of dread, you're completely exhausted and overwhelmed. You're juggling it all, work, family, and a mountain of personal responsibilities. The weight of it all makes you feel like you're barely keeping your head above water. You're exhausted, but you keep pushing yourself because that's what you think you have to do. The idea of asking for help never really crosses your mind, after all, you've always handled everything on your own.

Now, imagine this scenario. You wake up every morning feeling happy, light, and refreshed because you've done the work and learned to recognize when you need support and you aren't afraid to ask for it. You openly share your struggles with your closest friends and your family who know how to help you lighten your load. You've built a bad*** network of support that you can't imagine how you lived without. You feel more connected to yourself, way less stressed, and you are genuinely happy with your life. Let's explore together how to Bsupported and transform your life.

Bsupported comes in many shapes and sizes, touching every aspect of our lives. It could be emotional, practical, or even professional. Having people to lean on doesn't just make life easier; it fundamentally improves our ability to handle life's ups and downs. Recognizing when and how to ask for help isn't just a handy skill—it's essential. Yet, it's something we often only think about when we're already feeling swamped and overwhelmed.

Many of Us Struggle Silently—You Don't Have To

In a world that values self-sufficiency and independence, so many women struggle silently for whatever reasons may B, it's common for us bad*** women to bear all our burdens alone, mistakenly equating solitude with strength. However, the truth is far different. Keeping our struggles to ourselves can cause a range of mental, emotional, and physical issues. If you get one thing out of this chapter, we want you to know that it's ok to struggle, we all do, but it is also crucial to realize that asking for help and opening up about your feelings isn't a sign of weakness—it's actually a super brave and wise choice. We can't emphasize this enough—talk about your struggles with someone, ask for help when you need it and please get out of your head.

The Dangers of Isolation

We all know at least one person who isolates during hard times. Maybe it's your best friend or sister, or maybe it's you. You don't want to burden anyone with your problems, they have their own shit to deal with right? You stuff it down and think, well here's another thing I have to deal with. The weight of everything piling up feels crushing so instead of doing anything, you do nothing. You clam up and feel depressed and ashamed for even being in this situation in the first place. You don't want anyone else knowing what a screw-up you are. Well, let us tell you something. Get that shit out of your head. You are loved, you are worthy, and you are supported.

Isolation can be a silent predator, quietly sneaking into our lives under the guise of resilience. When we choose to deal with our problems alone, we miss out on the valuable insights and support that others can offer that could provide the relief and solutions we crave. Over time, this can lead to more anxiety, depression, and a feeling of being overwhelmed by life.

If you are in a habit of isolating to cope, it may be hard to start coming out of your head. You will have tugging feelings that want you to creep back into yourself and say forget it. You will be very vulnerable for a while, but it will get better. Vulnerability is not a bad thing.

Studies have shown that individuals who keep their struggles to themselves are more likely to experience a decline in mental health and overall happiness. A study shared in the Journal of Health and Social Behavior found that when people open up about their emotions, they're actually less stressed and feel better mentally.[8] So there's some solid science behind the idea that sharing how we feel, and Bsupported not only feels good but is good for us.

The Power of Vulnerability

Sharing our emotions, fears, and dreams does more than lighten our emotional load. I know it can feel scary, but It helps make the hard days, weeks, or seasons of our life much more manageable.. Embracing our vulnerability in the right time deepens our connections with ourselves and others if we let it. It invites deeper connections and strengthens our bonds with the people in our lives. This can be in our personal relationships, professional environments, and even our casual acquaintances.

Sharing As a Tool for Managing Mental Health

Opening up also plays a crucial role in managing our mental health. Talking about our dreams and fears has therapeutic effects, serving as a form of verbal processing that helps us untangle through and organize our thoughts that might otherwise remain knotted and unresolved. By giving voice to our inner feelings and desires, we create a narrative that is easy to understand and navigate. For example, when we share our aspirations with friends or

---

8   Mushtaq, R., Shoib, S., Shah, T., and Mushtaq, S. (2014). "Relationship between Loneliness, Psychiatric Disorders and Physical Health? A Review on the Psychological Aspects of Loneliness." *Journal of Clinical and Diagnostic Research: JCDR, 8*(9), WE01–WE4. https://doi.org/10.7860/JCDR/2014/10077.4828.

mentors, we not only gain feedback but often discover new insights and receive encouragement that pushes us to move forward.

It is clear that staying silent about our struggles does more harm than good. By embracing vulnerability and opening up to others, we do so much more than lighten our own load, we also invite others to understand and support us in our journey. As we continue to explore this chapter, we will explore deeper into learning to recognize when we need support, the best way to ask for it, and why it is so important to build a support network around us.

Knowing When You Need Support

Understanding when to seek support is so important for nurturing our mental and emotional sanity. We overlook the blatant signs of distress, blowing them off as nothing we haven't been through before, as a temporary stress, or just a minor setback. However, getting good at identifying these signs and doing something about them early will prevent more severe issues down the line. Look at this list, do you recognize any of these?

Signs That Signal the Need for Support
- **Persistent Sadness or Anxiety:** When feelings of sadness or anxiety become a constant background noise in your life, it's a sign that you might need to reach out for support.
- **Overwhelm and Emotional Exhaustion:** When you're constantly feeling overwhelmed and/or tired, even after rest, it suggests the burden you're carrying might be too heavy to manage alone.
- **Irritability and Mood Swings:** Frequent sudden changes in your mood or unexpected irritability can be signs that your emotional burdens are taking a toll on your mental health.

- **Physical Symptoms:** Chronic stress can manifest physically. If you are experiencing symptoms such as headaches, sleep disturbances, or a weakened immune system, these could be signs that your body is under too much stress.
- **Withdrawal from Social Activities:** If you find yourself pulling away from your friends, family, or activities you usually enjoy, When the thought of social interactions becomes draining or you start withdrawing from relationships it might be a sign that you're struggling more than you realize.
- **Cognitive Impairments:** If you are having consistent difficulty concentrating, you're forgetting everything, or you are having trouble making decisions all point to an overloaded mind in need of support.

Tuning into these signs, you can take proactive steps to Bsupported when you need it. We promise you it will help your emotional wellness. Here are some helpful tools to use to evaluate where you are now.

Self-Assess

- **Journaling:** Keeping a daily journal is a powerful way to track your emotions and spot patterns signaling a need for support. It allows for a quiet pause in your day to process feelings and thoughts.
- **Mindfulness and Reflection:** Practicing mindfulness can help in becoming more attuned to your emotional state. Regular reflection can alert you to consistent feelings of being off-balance, guiding you to seek support when needed.
- **Feedback from People You Trust:** Sometimes, it's hard to see the signs of stress and overwhelm in ourselves because

we are in it too deep. Asking a close friend or family member for their honest observations can provide you with insight into whether you might need support.

Often, the signs that suggest a need for external help can be subtle or overlooked until they manifest into more significant issues. If you don't get adequate support, you'll wind up with a tampon stuck in your vagina . . . more than once.

Chrissy

Yes, ugh, you read that right. So one day I went to see my ob-gyn because something was not right—it didn't smell right, didn't feel right, something was very wrong downstairs. Well, I found out I had forgotten to remove a tampon from my last period. She removed it, and everything was fine (besides being completely mortified).

The very next month I was convinced I did it again. I couldn't remember if I took it out, I couldn't find one, and since the symptoms weren't as dramatic as the month before, I dreaded the thought of going back to the same doctor. I talked to Danny: I think I did it again.

Chrissy, in all your years, you've never done this, what is going on? You're overwhelmed, you're doing too much," etc. "Get Your cop flashlight and meet me in the closet."

So there I was lying on the floor in our bedroom closet with my legs spread and he had his light shining into my vagina. As I stared at the ceiling, feeling highly awkward about how Danny was seeing me in this vulnerable state, a thought struck me: Chrissy, what is going on? You gotta slow down. Your self-care is so in the negative zone that you're forgetting if you've removed your tampon. Twice!

That was the moment I realized I needed a bit more self-care. Thank you, Danny.

Acknowledging the signs, accepting that you need support, and opening up to receive it are not admissions of defeat but rather the opposite. They are signs of self-awareness and strength. The next logical step after recognizing these signs is learning how to effectively communicate your needs.

In the following sections, we will talk about practical advice on how to voice your needs for support, ensuring that you can convey your feelings and requests clearly and effectively to those around you.

How to Ask for Help

We understand that you may rather sit on a cactus than ask for help but trust us, it is essential for managing life's challenges and maintaining your mental and emotional sanity. Knowing how and when to approach others effectively will make a big difference in the response and support you receive.

First things first, focus on the one thing. You can start small; start with acknowledging your need for a ten-minute bath and let your partner know they'll need to watch the kids. Or maybe acknowledge your need for friend time and call a friend to come over and watch a movie in your pajamas.

Choose the Right Moment and Setting

Choose a time when the person you are asking for help is not rushed or distracted. You want to make sure they can give you their full attention. Find a place that is private and comfortable for both of you to open up and have an honest heart-to-heart.

You Have to Be Clear and Specific About Your Needs

Use clear words to articulate what you are feeling and what you need. For example, "I've been feeling really overwhelmed with the house lately and could use help organizing the kids' closets." Be specific about the support you need. Maybe it's emotional support, practical help, or professional advice, whatever it is you have to help the other person understand how best to support you. Clear communication helps prevent misunderstandings that can lead to frustration for both of you.

Express Vulnerability

Be Honest: Sharing your vulnerabilities can be powerful if you open up to it. Let them know that asking for help is challenging for you and express appreciation for their support.

Chrissy

Danny supported me through my mortifying tampon crisis, but he didn't stop there. And I decided that I needed to support myself too, from that moment I knew I needed to learn to take better care of myself. I needed to see self-care as good for me, good for my health, and good for my family and not see it as selfish any longer. More importantly, I needed to know how to ask for what I needed like I had to ask Danny to grab the flashlight and meet me in the closet. "Whatever you need, let me know."

Danny became my accountability person. Here's the plan. I'm going to do something every week that is just for me. I'll take a long bath, I'll take a power nap, instead of jumping on the trampoline with the kids, I'll go get my nails done, etc. I'll do whatever I want, whatever I enjoy and that's okay.

Now I have self-care Mondays, I can work from home, organize something at home, go explore a new place or new restaurant or store, get a massage, and I have the world at my feet. Don't get me wrong, sometimes I forget and start doing too much work on those days, but I always pull myself back. Let me tell you something, Life feels so much better now, it feels…lighter. I am better at taking time for self-care, I'm a better mom and a better wife, and my family is living better for it, too.

If you have forgotten how to take care of yourself like I did for so long, I am here to support you. If you have a question, please, please don't struggle in silence—reach out, feel free to email me! I'll do my best to B there for you. Add Rae and I to your support network and know that you are right where you need to be right now.

Show Your Gratitude

Our Mom, Cathy, shows her love through home-cooked meals and quality time. Every Tuesday, after caring for her grandkids all day, she piles food on all our plates. And she has a lot of love in her Italian heart, which means there is a LOT of food. Our Mom makes family dinner every Tuesday night and packs up leftovers. This means every week, we have one night where we don't have to think about dinner, and our lunches are taken care of for the next day.

We're immensely grateful when we walk into her kitchen every Tuesday it's absolute chaos. The house is filled with eight cousins loving each other's company, yelling, running, and filling every room.

In these moments, we feel taken care of. She cooked dinner for all of us, we got to just walk in, make a plate, and not think . . . and the kids were so happy. Most people don't even get together for holidays with their whole family, and we get to on Tuesday nights.

Her love extends way beyond Tuesday dinners, though. She will also drop off a meal or bring over soup if we're sick. When we had our babies, mom moved in with us for a week and reminded us that our job was to heal and feed the baby. She took care of everything else. Mom seems to know what we need in those moments without us asking. These things continually remind me of her warmth and we are so blessed for the security her support brings. Thanks Mom.

We know not everyone has a Mom like ours, but that's why you need to focus on building a support system of people you can be real with. We have one another, and are blessed to have friends we can be no-filter with and say whatever is on our minds.

Always express your gratitude for the time and assistance others give you. You're not only showing you respect them but also encouraging them to be supportive in the future. Appreciate the everyday acts of kindness around you, you will not only nurture your relationships, but you will also keep up a cycle of kindness and care.

Offer Reciprocity

Mutual Support: Let them know that you are there for them as well. Support is a two-way street, and offering your assistance in return can strengthen your relationship.

Asking for help is a skill that benefits from practice. The more you do it, the more natural it will become, enhancing your ability to maintain strong and supportive relationships.

Barriers to Support

Many of us hesitate to ask for help due to whatever barriers but understanding and addressing the obstacles can help ease the process of finding and accepting support when we need it. Perhaps you can relate to one or two of these.

Pride and Independence

Recognize the Strength in Vulnerability: Understand that asking for help is a sign of self-awareness and strength, not weakness. Sharing your struggles can lead to deeper connections and more effective solutions.

Start Small: If you're uncomfortable asking for help, start with small, manageable requests as you build comfort and trust in others' willingness to assist.

Fear of Vulnerability

Confidentiality Concerns: Choose trustworthy people who respect privacy to confide in, creating a safe space to share your concerns.

Gradual Disclosure: Share your feelings and needs gradually to manage the fear of being judged or rejected. This also helps others understand your situation better, enabling them to offer appropriate support.

Lack of Knowledge

Educate Yourself: Sometimes, not knowing how to seek help or what resources are available can be a significant barrier. Take time to research local resources, support groups, or counseling services.

Ask for Guidance: If you're unsure where to start, ask close friends or professionals for recommendations on support options that could suit your needs.

Overwhelm and Desperation

Prioritize Your Needs: When overwhelmed, prioritize your immediate needs and tackle them one at a time.

Seek Professional Help: Professionals can provide structured support and guidance, helping to manage feelings of overwhelm effectively.

By confronting these barriers with practical strategies and a mindset geared toward growth and support, and accessing the help we need, we're on the way to improved well-being and resilience.

Your Support Network

Support can come when you ask for it and it can come in any number of directions, and then sometimes support comes from a place you least expect it. When we started our Power to B brand, Dad said nothing. It started from our fertility journey, which is something he wouldn't talk about so he didn't. But then it turned into jewelry, his comfort zone, business, etc. Big Lew, one of those guys who can fix anything, can solve any problem, he can make beautiful jewelry with his bare hands, and always shows up when you need him. He just doesn't always know how to handle emotional conversations and gets skittish around "female" issues.

We had some momentum with The Power to B, and all of a sudden he understood what we were doing and saw that it was more than just a bracelet. In the conversations we were having, customers were talking about how it was impacting their lives positively.

He came to us one morning.

"I woke up in the middle of the night and I wrote inspirational "Power poems" he called them, for each of the Powerwords."

He started reading the poems aloud to us.

That was the first time we realized he was supporting us in the actual goal—this passion project, not just the money-making side of it.

We felt seen, understood, and so supported.

I don't really know if Dad knows how powerful this moment was for us, and how seeing the tangible evidence of his support spurred us forward. Thanks Dad.

Finding support where you don't expect it requires you to combine Bopen, with Bsupported. There is support available to you in your life, you just might not be recognizing it or taking advantage of it. This brings us to the next step in Bsupported.

Creating Your Support Network

Your support network needs to include many different types of people because no one person can offer you every type of support you need.

Rae

My closest friend (who is also named Chrissy) is also an entrepreneur and a mom, and the bond we share is something truly special. In family businesses (which are both a part of) it's easy to feel as if no one really understands the unique pressures and challenges that come along with building and growing a company. But with her, it's different. She gets me in a way that others simply can't. We speak the same language, share a similar drive, and understand the rollercoaster of emotions that come with being an entrepreneur and mom—the busy minds, the relentless pursuit of our goals, and the occasional self-doubt that creeps in.

In her, I find not just a friend but a confidante who knows what it's like to face the highs and lows of entrepreneurship. When I'm struggling, she's there with advice that comes from a place of genuine understanding, and when I'm celebrating a win, she's cheering the loudest because she knows exactly how much it means. I offer her the same in return—a mutual support system that's built on trust, respect, and a shared vision for success. In a world where so many people don't quite understand the entrepreneurial journey, having her by my side makes all the difference. Together, we navigate the challenges, celebrate the victories, and push each other to keep going, knowing that we're never truly alone in our endeavors.

Combining the support from her with the support from my sister Chrissy and my husband—my life is full of people who are real, strong, and a huge positive influence in my life.

Creating a support network is vital not just for personal growth but also for navigating the challenges of living life. First, you have to know what you need support for. Let me show you how we navigate looking for support.

Get something to write on. Don't do this in your head. Use your journal, a computer, paper, your notes app, or something. And get this on paper where you can evaluate it with some distance, some perspective, and get it out of your head.

Steps for seeking support

1. **Become aware that you need something:** If you're feeling exhausted, have a short fuse, etc. you need to jump out of the river of life and take a break.

2. **Figure out why you feel overloaded:** What feels hard right now? Women struggle a lot with thinking that there is one magic answer or one magic thing that will solve their problems. There is no magic pill. I want one, we all do, and we keep looking for it—but that's not how life is, it's always small tweaks and changes that lead to more joy. It's more like sections of shifting. One small move at a time, micro shifts.

3. **Brainstorm:** What's one small thing I can do? You have to pick one thing, otherwise you'll feel scattered. You can do it all, but you can't do it all at one time. Be honest with yourself about how much you can do, and what's most important, and create the momentum that you need.

4. **Find a person who can support you:** First, ask yourself, do you know someone who . . . whatever the thing you need. Who supported me in the past? Who can I reach out to to talk about this problem? Who is available to support me now? Ask for other people's ideas too, people you trust can help you figure out the next right thing to do. LISTEN to these people, learn, and find one thing you can take from the conversations.

> **Chrissy**

So, right now, I need a babysitter because Danny and I aren't getting enough date nights. I can feel the disconnect and it doesn't feel good. Ironically enough, I just spent time talking to my ghostwriter about this problem, and she was feeling it too in her marriage.

Here's what I am struggling with. Finding a babysitter I can trust. We have a pool in the backyard and I worry about leaving my kids with a random person from Care.com. My kids are too important to leave them with someone I don't even know. This is one thing I won't budge on. I need someone I have built a relationship with to help me with this.

My ghostwriter lives nearby and has a twenty-two-year-old daughter who wants to make extra money—I got her number and suddenly had a summer babysitter who was a certified lifeguard and former camp counselor. Isn't that something? The universe always has a way of bringing you the answers you need. All I did was talk about what I needed.

Cultivating Meaningful Relationships

Focus on fostering deeper connections with fewer people rather than trying to maintain a large number of acquaintances. If the relationship takes away your energy instead of fueling you, it's probably not the right person to offer you support. That doesn't mean you can't be there for this person, but it does mean it's not a person you can Bsupported by.

Be Proactive: Don't wait for others to reach out; take the initiative to set up meetings, check in regularly, and offer help when others are in need.

Leveraging Community Resources

Engage with Local Groups: Try to find something local you connect with. Whether it's a book club, a knitting group, or a volunteer organization, actively participating in your community can lead to meaningful interactions and support.

Utilize Community Centers: These often provide various programs that can offer both direct support and opportunities to meet people with similar interests.

Building Professional Networks

Attend Industry Meetups and Conferences: These can be excellent places to meet like-minded professionals who can offer career guidance and support.

Join Professional Associations: Being a part of professional bodies can not only help in career development but also provide a safety net during industry downturns. You can never really have too many connections.

Embracing Online Social Networks

Join Relevant Online Communities: Platforms like LinkedIn, Facebook groups, or specialty forums can be a good place for connecting with people who share similar interests or challenges.

Be Active and Supportive Online: If you prefer to find support online, regular participation and engagement in discussions can build your profile as a supportive and reliable member of the community.

If you invest a little time and effort into some of these strategies, you can build a network that not only supports you in the hard times but also enriches your daily life, providing you with a well-rounded foundation of resources and relationships to reach out to.

In this chapter, we explored the multifaceted nature of support, emphasizing its importance in our lives. From recognizing when you need help to asking when you need to, to effectively building a support network, each step is meant to present a resilient and supportive environment for yourself and others around you.

> RemindHer: You are never alone; reach out and lean on your community when you need it.

CHAPTER 11

Bkind

Part One—Bkind to Yourself

Kindness isn't just a nice thing. It's a powerful force that can change your life and the lives of those around you. Bkind is a two-part initiative. We'll first explore how being kind to yourself can make a big difference. Next, we'll see how self-care creates a ripple effect of positivity that impacts others. It is possible to create a world that's happier, more compassionate, and more connected. So, let's begin with Bkind to yourself.

Rae

I keep repeating the phrase "Be kind to yourself" in my head these days. When I'm feeling tired, stressed, overwhelmed, I tend to lose the inclination to be kind and become my own worst critic. I remember the time I returned home from a trip (not vacation, that's a different vibe). I felt tired this week. I was in the process of booking a photo shoot for the book cover and I said to myself:

I'm doing this photo shoot in two months, how skinny can I get in two months? I asked myself this not because I feel like I need to lose weight but because I was feeling tired and haven't taken care to be kind to myself. I journaled that morning and had to change my mindset: My affirmations that day were to give myself grace and take a walk. I made it a point to take time to take care of myself so I can stop being mean to myself for no other reason than because I was feeling tired.

My usual body mindset is gratitude for what my body can do for me, the exercise I am able to do, and the children it carries. etc. But, when I'm not taking good care of myself, I forget and slip back into old habits. I called Chrissy and said "I'm so excited about the photo shoot, but I have to tell you how dark my head went for moment. Do you have an inner mean girl? What does she say? When does she show up? What is something you can do to quiet her down?"

Once I took the time to take care of myself, it helped reset my brain. I know this mean girl is louder when everyone is demanding more of me than I have to give so I have to set boundaries, stop answering the phone, stop responding to text messages, and get back into my routine, I came back from the trip with an enormous pile of need from family, kids, work, obligations. That same week when I was taking control of getting back into a routine and regaining my self-care, my sister called with an extra ticket to a concert with a group of girlfriends. Deep down, I had major FOMO. Then the realization set in that I knew that what I really needed was an evening to myself after the kids were in bed to meditate, stretch, drink tea, read a magazine, watch a mindless show and release how I've been feeling. I needed to stop being a machine. Women are machines, and sometimes that machine breaks if we don't do regular maintenance. I skipped my regular maintenance the week prior and so, now I needed to have a 'me moment. So, with confidence, I called my sister, explained to her how I was feeling and I rejected the extra ticket and did what was right for me.

Simple Steps for a Happier You

It's easy to get caught up in a busy day, go through our usual habits, and forget about being nice to ourselves. Yet, it's one of the most important things you can do. Here are a few things you can do to get started on your Bkind project.

Nurture Your Inner Voice

When you speak kindly to yourself, you're giving yourself the nutrients you need to blossom into something beautiful. Being kind to others begins with growing love and compassion in your own life. It begins with speaking kindly to yourself.

Decide to Be Kind

Decide that being nice to yourself is a big deal. It's not just saying you'll do it, but showing determination to live it out. Think about how you treat your best friends. You deserve the same kindness.

Stop Being Hard on Yourself

The first step of being kind might be to stop being unkind. Everybody has bad days, but learn to give yourself a break. Mistakes are lessons, not a license to beat yourself up. A little self-compassion goes a long way.

Find Simple Rituals

Little things can make a big difference. For example, making yourself a cup of tea can be more than just a drink—it can be a moment to relax and feel good. Finding these small rituals can help you feel better, even on tough days.

So next time you're feeling down, check your mindset. Show yourself compassion, and speak kindly to yourself. You deserve it!

RemindHer

Prompts can be a great way to keep us on track. Placing reminders in our daily surroundings can be highly effective. Let's explore how these reminders can help us change how we talk to ourselves and cultivate a mindset of self-love.

RemindHer Objects

Wearing a Bkind bracelet can be a game-changer. It's a simple reminder to be kind and empathetic, not just to others but to yourself, too. For many people, wearing the bracelet has led to feeling happier, more positive, and more connected to others.

Setting Up Your RemindHer Space

Imagine setting aside a special spot in your room, maybe by your mirror, where you put up reminders of self-kindness. You can use a dry-erase marker on the mirror to write down promises to yourself, like "I will be kind to myself." These reminders act as a gentle push to treat yourself with love and care, even on tough days.

Changing How We See Ourselves

When we look in the mirror, it's easy to notice things we don't like about our appearance. So, watch how you talk to yourself. Remind yourself that perfection is never required, then give positivity equal time. Find at least one thing you like about your appearance, and take the time to focus on that quality.

Meet Yourself Halfway: Balancing Self-Care

Life can get pretty hectic, making it tough to take care of yourself, but there are plenty of ways to give yourself a break. Let's explore some ways to prioritize self-care, even when schedules are tight.

Get Creative with Self-Care

When a full day off isn't possible, think outside the box. Can you spare an hour for yourself? Maybe you can sneak in a short walk or enjoy a relaxing bath while the kids have some screen time. It's all about finding small moments to recharge.

Take Mini Breaks

Even in the middle of a busy day, it's crucial to pause and take care of yourself. A quick stroll around the block or a few minutes of quiet time is all it takes to make a difference. These mini breaks can help you feel refreshed and ready to tackle whatever comes your way.

Do One Thing You Love

No matter how busy you are, make time for something you enjoy every day. It could be as simple as listening to your favorite song or treating yourself to a small snack. Focus your attention on those moments and savor them.

Embrace Imperfection

Self-care isn't about being perfect. It's okay if you can't do it all or if things don't go as planned. Give yourself permission to care for yourself, even if it means meeting yourself halfway. Effort counts, and tiny steps take you toward self-care.

Move to Neutral

Self-kindness doesn't always have to be about big, positive statements. Sometimes, it's okay to keep things simple. Moving to neutral can be a step in the right direction. We spoke with Georgia Homsany, author of *You're Not Lazy*, and founder & CEO of Daily Dose Wellness. She shared some ideas for moving from negative self-talk to neutral self-talk as a stepping stone for the positivity we want to cultivate.

Homsany said when you think a negative thought, you can replace it with a reframed idea about the same thing. Your words become your thoughts, which then becomes your reality. If you can stick with it and stick with reframing negative thoughts you will begin to feel differently. Our words impact our lives.

If you say: "I'm fat," first, catch yourself and say something neutral such as: "I have a body," state the facts without positive or negative judgment attached. Once that's comfortable, then try to tell yourself something positive:" I have beautiful hair," "My eyes are really pretty," or something else you believe. Alternatively, reframe those thoughts into something positive by saying, for example, "I'm voluptuous" instead of "I'm fat"; acknowledge your curves, but turn them into a positive thing instead of a negative thing.

You can also reframe your thoughts with logic. If you think to yourself, "I am a bad mom because I'm always nagging my daughter," reframe that by saying, 1) "I'm asking my daughter to do this because I care," 2) say something neutral such as "I am a mom," and then 3) "I care about my daughter so I ask things of her" instead of "I am a nag." The shift of focus from negative to neutral, and eventually to positive, is so important. There are many benefits of reframing one's thoughts, such as positively affecting your self-esteem and positively perceiving how you show up every day in the world.

If you're constantly putting yourself down, you will have low self-worth and in turn, feeling inadequate will make you show up without your full potential. Your words become your thoughts and thoughts become your reality. If you can rework those negative thoughts your self-worth will improve, you will show up more energetically in the world, and your reality will improve.

On days when positive thinking feels tough, it's okay to shift to a neutral mindset. Instead of aiming for big affirmations, think about the simple facts. For instance, consider how your eyes help you see and read. It's a neutral truth that can still bring a sense of appreciation for what you have.

Self-care doesn't have to be complicated. Little things matter, too. For example, placing a cold washcloth on your eyes can be a quick way to relax and relieve stress. It may not bring you to a positive place, but it is a step away from the negative.

Don't underestimate the impact of small acts of kindness toward yourself. Whether it's appreciating the functionality of your body or doing something simple to relax, these actions add up. They remind you that you're worthy of love and attention, even when things aren't perfect. So, next time you're struggling with positivity, don't fight it. Do something small to move to neutral. In time, the positivity will come.

Move Your Body

When we think about being kind to ourselves, it's easy to forget about the role of physical activity. Yet moving our bodies isn't just good for staying fit. It's also great for our mental health and self-care. Let's explore how exercise can help us feel better mentally and emotionally.

A Bkind Body

Taking time to move your body is like giving it a big hug. Going for a walk, doing yoga, dancing around your room, or any other form of exercise shows your body some love.

The Feel-Good Chemicals

When you exercise, your body releases chemicals called endorphins. These little guys are like natural mood boosters. They help you feel happier and more relaxed and can even ease any aches or pains you might have.

Exercise As a Mental Break

Ever notice how your worries seem to fade away when you're working out? That's because exercise gives your brain a break from all the stress and chatter. Instead of worrying about tomorrow or that argument with your friend, you're focused on how your body feels right now.

Finding Joy in Movement

Being kind to yourself doesn't mean you have to slog through a boring workout. It's all about finding activities that you enjoy. Whether shooting hoops with friends, going for a bike ride or trying out a new dance routine, Bkind exercise should be fun.

Keep Track of the Kindness

We may be able to find Bkind support in how others treat us. Pay attention to the nice things people say and hold onto the uplifting interactions. Kind words can lift your spirits. Let's explore simple ways to gather and use these positive messages to boost our Bkind mindset.

Remembering Kind Words

One easy way to keep track of the nice things others say is by writing them down. You can have a special section in your journal or use an area in a "Power to B" journal. Whenever someone says something nice about you, jot it down. These words can be a real source of comfort when you need a pick-me-up.

Surprises from Loved Ones

Imagine waking up to find a message on your mirror from your kids, a note from your spouse, or a card from a friend. These acts of kindness can make your day. Take a moment to appreciate these messages and let them sink in. They're a reminder of the love and support around you.

Creating Your Encouragement Album

You can also create an album on your phone filled with uplifting messages. Collect compliments, achievements, and words of encouragement from friends and family. Take a look through this album to remind yourself of your strengths and the people who believe in you.

Asking for Support

It's totally okay to ask for a compliment when you're feeling down. Reach out to the people who care about you and ask for their support and kind words. Hearing a few nice things from a friend or family member can really make a difference.

Finding Community Support

If you don't have a strong support system, consider joining a community. Being around people who uplift and encourage each other can be a huge help for your mental and emotional well-being. If you don't have them already, seek them out.

Use "I Feel" Statements

The words we use matter. Often, we define ourselves by how we're feeling at the moment. For example, if we wake up feeling slow or unenergetic, we might say, "I am lazy." This can be unfair and not true. Instead, we can try saying, "I feel tired." This way, we acknowledge the feeling without making it who we are.

Challenging Negative Thoughts

Using "I feel" statements can also help us deal with negative thoughts. Instead of believing we're lazy or tired all the time, we realize that these feelings come and go. For example, feeling tired after a bad night's sleep isn't laziness—it's just a natural reaction to not getting enough rest. So by saying "I feel tired," we're kinder to ourselves.

Understanding Your Feelings

Using "I feel" statements helps us understand ourselves better. It reminds us that our feelings change, and that's okay. Accept those feelings without judgment and explore the reasons behind them.

Stop, Rest, Reset

A prime reason for negativity is fatigue. Many people are pushing themselves non-stop. That is a bad habit and needs to be addressed. It's okay to stop and rest when we need to. Let's explore why it's essential to listen to our bodies and prioritize rest, even when we feel pressured to keep going.

Taking a Breather

Sometimes, we need to hit the pause button and give ourselves a break. It's not about giving up or being lazy. It's about knowing our limits and taking care of ourselves. Pushing ourselves too hard only leads to feeling worn out and overwhelmed. It's important to recognize when we've done enough and give ourselves permission to rest.

Even when there's a lot to do, pushing ourselves too much isn't healthy. We should replace self-criticism with words of encouragement. Say things like, "That's enough for today. Good job and tomorrow is another day."

Checking Our Pace

It's easy to get caught up in the rush of life and forget to slow down. Keep an eye on how fast you're going. If you're pushing yourself too hard, it's okay to take a step back and relax. Pay attention to how we're feeling to prevent burnout and stay balanced.

Try Something New

When it comes to being kind to ourselves, staying curious is a powerful tool. Be playful, have fun, and embrace the adventure of life. It helps us avoid negativity. Let's explore why curiosity matters and why fun is a must.

Why Curiosity Is Key

Curiosity acts like a guide, leading us to new discoveries and growth. Instead of getting stuck in negative thoughts, it encourages us to see the world with wonder and enthusiasm.

Adding Playfulness

Being playful goes hand in hand with curiosity. It brings joy and spontaneity into our lives, helping us face life in a light-hearted way.

A Fun Activity

Having trouble thinking of something fun? Here are a few ideas to get your creativity flowing:

- Try a New Recipe
- Draw or Doodle
- Watch Funny Videos
- DIY Craft
- Read a Short Story or Poem
- Play a Quick Game
- Coloring
- Meditation or Deep Breathing
- Call or Video Chat with a Friend
- Photography
- Puzzle Time
- Watch the Sunset or Sunrise
- Write in a Journal
- Listen to Music or a Podcast
- Go Cloud Watching

It really doesn't matter what it is. Just relax and have fun.

Track Your Cycle

Knowing your body's natural rhythm can be a game-changer for taking care of yourself. By keeping tabs on your menstrual cycle and how you feel at different times, you can better meet your body's needs and stay healthy.

By tracking your menstrual cycle, you learn a lot about yourself. You can see patterns in your mood and energy levels, helping you figure out what your body needs to feel its best.

Your body sends you signals all the time. Maybe you're feeling tired and need a nap, or perhaps you're craving a snack for a boost. Tune into these signals and take action, like going for a run or grabbing some water. Give your body what it needs to stay healthy and happy.

Understanding your body and giving it what it needs is a power move. It's all about taking control of your health and feeling empowered. So, start tracking your cycle and embracing the wisdom of your body.

The Benefits of Treating Yourself Kindly

Chrissy

Being good to yourself isn't just a nice idea. It can make a huge difference in your life. I used to let the number on the scale control my mood for the day. It was tough and left me feeling defeated. But now, I've changed my approach. I focus on drinking water, eating healthy, and squeezing in a quick walk, even if it's short. This shift in mindset has brought me to a kinder place. Here are some Bkind benefits:

Finding Joy in Small Moments

By being kinder to myself, I've found more joy in everyday things, like joking around with my kids. It's made me feel more energetic and positive throughout the day.

Overcoming Worries

I used to get anxious about things like spending money, but I've learned to challenge those worries and trust in myself. I've realized that I can always make more money and have what it takes to figure things out. This has given me the confidence to invest in things that matter to me.

The Ripple Effect

Treating myself kindly has changed everything. It's changed how I face challenges, how I interact with others, and how I feel about myself. It has set the stage for a happier, more fulfilling life.

From feeling happier and more confident to handling challenges better, Bkind is a game-changer, and it begins with yourself. Bkind to yourself will naturally lead to the second phase of the Bkind journey—Bkind to others.

Part Two—Bkind to Others

We created the Bkind bracelet while the world was recovering from COVID and human connection seemed to be waning. The world seemed at odds with one another and more focused on combativeness than connection. We wanted to create a reminder to Bkind to one another because you never know what someone is going through.

The more love you give to people, the more you will get in return. If you empathize and think about things from other people's perspectives, you will get that positive energy back ten fold. This Powerword is the RemindHer to love, give what you want to receive, and that you have the opportunity to make someone else's day.

Rae

I love showing kindness in small ways like paying for someone's coffee, sending unexpected texts expressing my gratitude to someone, bringing treats to the kids teams during sporting events and other small acts that light everybody up. I love to give people compliments—even strangers. Small gestures add up to big feelings. All of my businesses are retail. We have a showroom, and it feels like we are inviting people into our homes every day. I try to live and work by the saying that people will not remember the things you say, but they will remember the way you make them feel.

Taking care of ourselves doesn't just benefit us; it affects everyone around us. When we practice self-care activities, we become better equipped to handle stress and navigate life's challenges. When we're more balanced and centered, we're better able to provide support, empathy, and understanding to those around us.

When we prioritize self-care, we demonstrate the value of self-love and self-respect. This can be particularly impactful for children and young adults who learn from observing the behavior of adults in their lives. By showing them that it's essential to prioritize their own well-being, we empower them to develop healthy habits that will serve them well throughout their lives.

When well-rested, energized, and emotionally balanced, we're more productive and creative. This can positively impact our family life, work environment, and community activities. By taking care of ourselves, we contribute to a positive and productive atmosphere, inspiring others to do the same.

As I have worked on this in my own life, I can share with you what a difference it has made in the most important areas of my life.

> For our kids.

Chrissy

When I make time for self-care, I can fully engage with my kids. I'm not hesitant to playfully jump on the trampoline with my kids, even if it means I pee my pants a little. It strengthens our bond and creates special moments together.

Rae

Taking care of myself helps me stay calm and patient, even when things get hectic. Instead of getting frustrated with my kids, I can handle it with grace and find a solution to whatever household disaster we are facing at that moment.

> For our husbands.

Chrissy

Self-care also benefits my relationship with my husband. When I prioritize my well-being, I have more energy to spend quality time with him. It may be sitting by the fire or sending a flirty text during the day. When I feel good because of my self-care, I'm not so consumed with myself. I can be more attentive to him.

> For our colleagues.

Taking care of yourself isn't just about personal relationships. It impacts your professional life, too. As leaders and mentors, self-care makes us more creative, confident, and compassionate towards our colleagues, leading to better teamwork and communication. It helps us approach conversations with empathy and fairness, creating a positive and more supportive work environment.

Being kind to ourselves has a ripple effect on everyone around us. By prioritizing self-care, we not only improve our own lives but also create happier, healthier relationships and workplaces.

Taking Action

You don't have to wait until you've got everything figured out to start being kind to others. We can all spread kindness, even if we're still learning to be kind to ourselves. Let's take some time to explore why it's important to take action and be kind to others, no matter where we are on our journey.

Kindness Flows Both Ways

Being kind to yourself is a process, and it's okay if you're still working on it. In fact, being kind to others can help you become kinder to yourself. It's good practice, and the positive feedback you receive can help you build momentum for self-care.

The Power of Doing Something

Taking action to be kind to others makes someone else's day better and creates a positive vibe for everyone around. Whether it's a smile, a compliment, or a small act of kindness, every little action counts.

Start Small, Start Now

You don't need to do something huge to spread kindness. It can be as simple as holding the door for someone or checking in on a friend. Start small, and see what comes as a result.

Be the Change You Want to See

If you want to live in a world full of kindness, you've got to start by being kind. By taking action and spreading kindness, you're helping to make the world a better place. Bkind to yourself. Bkind to others. Just Bkind.

By taking action and spreading kindness, you're making someone else's day brighter and improving your well-being. So, let's start now, one small act of kindness at a time, and watch as it spreads joy and positivity everywhere.

Start With the Little Things

Kindness doesn't always mean doing big things. Little things count and can lead to a big impact. Let's explore some small and easy ways to spread kindness every day.

Compliment Someone's Style

A simple compliment about someone's outfit can really make their day. Whether it's a friend or someone you just met, taking a moment to notice and appreciate their style can boost their confidence and spread positivity.

Pay It Forward with Coffee

Next time you're at the coffee shop, consider buying a coffee for the person behind you in line. It's a small gesture that can bring a smile to someone's face and create a chain reaction of kindness.

Say Thank You

Take a moment to send a text or write a note to someone you appreciate. Whether it's a friend, family member, or coworker, expressing gratitude can strengthen your bond and make both of you feel good.

Acknowledge Others' Efforts

Let your coworkers know that you appreciate their hard work. A little recognition can go a long way in making someone feel valued and motivated.

Surprise Someone With a Gift

Sending a surprise gift, like flowers or a book, is a thoughtful way to show someone you care. It doesn't have to be a special occasion. Small things can have a bigger impact when it's for no reason at all.

Share Laughter

Sharing a funny video or meme on social media is an easy way to spread joy. It's a simple gesture that can bring a smile to someone's face and make their day a little brighter.

Kindness doesn't have to be complicated. Incorporating these simple acts into our daily lives can make a positive impact and spread happiness in our little corner of the world. So, make it a habit and spread positivity wherever we go.

When You're Ready, Go Bigger

While small acts of kindness are great, sometimes it's the slightly bigger ones that really leave a mark on people. Once you've built up your Bkind momentum, you might be ready to go big. Let's dive into some thoughtful ways to show kindness that go a bit beyond the usual.

Invite Someone to Lunch

Taking the initiative to invite someone out to lunch and picking up the tab shows you appreciate their company. It's a chance to connect more deeply and strengthen your bond.

Cook a Meal for Someone

Putting effort into cooking a homemade meal for someone is a genuine way to show you care. Whether it's for a friend going through a rough patch or a neighbor who could use a break, the gesture won't go unnoticed.

Treat a Friend to a Wellness Session

Booking a massage, reiki session, or other wellness treatment for a friend is a caring way to help them relax. It demonstrates that you're invested in their well-being and want to support their self-care.

While small acts of kindness matter, the bigger ones can have an even greater impact. You're showing that you genuinely care and are willing to go the extra mile to make them feel special.

The Risks of Being Overly Kind

Being kind is admirable, but your Bkind life doesn't involve overdoing it and harming yourself. It is possible to be "kind to a fault," which can lead to stress and exhaustion. Here are some things to keep in mind on your Bkind journey.

Politeness vs. Genuine Kindness

Sometimes, we're nice even when we are being mistreated. Instead of being honest in a gentle way, we pretend to be okay. This might seem harmless, but it can build up and cause us stress.

Taking on Too Much

Being overly kind often means saying yes to everything. We end up with too much on our plate and feel overwhelmed, which can lead to burnout.

Nice versus Kind

Nice is surface level, it's general manners, but it's not letting your heart show. You can be nice and wish someone a happy birthday. You can be kind and say happy birthday, but also let the person know what makes them unique, or special. Our good friend's mom has sent us a message every year since we were kids. The message takes her less than five minutes to write, but getting it fills us with light and love. The message she sends makes our whole day—more than the gifts, the well wishes and anything else because this is a woman who has known us our whole lives and she takes that moment to pour into us. That's kindness.

In an effort to be nice, we could fail to set healthy boundaries. Kindness comes from the heart, but kindness also requires boundaries. Setting boundaries helps relationships stay healthy and balanced because they encourage fairness and mutual understanding. They prevent situations where a person might take advantage of us or ignore our feelings. Boundaries make it easier to trust each other, get closer, and feel safe in relationships.

We know a woman who never wanted to let other people down. She said yes to everything people asked of her at work, in the community, and in family and friendships. This level of people-pleasing depleted her and, once she became a mother and realized she was not leaving enough of herself for her family, she started to understand the power of boundaries. Do you see yourself in this story? Are you doing too much and feeling busy all the time? Setting some boundaries to protect your time can ensure that when you say yes to something it's coming from a place of kindness and love.

The Ramifications Are Huge

Chrissy

I keep a power word bracelet in my purse at all times. I'm ready to make an impact whenever I can. There have been times I gave a gift to a stranger. The bracelet always seems to find the right person at the right time, in a store, coffee shop, airport, or hotel.

I was once at a women's networking event and had a Bstrong bracelet in my purse. It was there for awhile. I was talking to a woman, and her eyes seemed sad to me. She was having problems in her business, but I could tell there was something else. During the conference, she'd write down notes and then sigh.

I could almost hear her thinking, "I can't do that."

I took a moment to write a note. At the end of the night, I went over to her and said I know we just met, but I have a present for you.

I gave her the note that read, "I think your business is amazing. I think maybe you haven't heard how awesome you're doing. I want to encourage you to keep going, stay strong, and wear this as a reminder."

Then I handed her the Powerword bracelet. She started crying.

If I can do something like this every day, it is a Bkind life. Maybe that gesture helped her and may inspire her to do something for someone else. When we find ways to make others feel seen, understood, and loved, we change the world.

Another example comes from the time we were in California at the Oscars gifting boutique. We were able to talk with Greg Tarzan Davis, Coyote in the new Top Gun movie, and help him choose a bracelet. He left a teaching career to pursue his dream of acting. We encouraged him to keep following his dreams. At the end of the event, he came up to us and asked for a hug. He had tears in his eyes, thanked us and said he felt a renewed sense of confidence in his path. Once in a while, we see him on social media wearing his bracelet and feel gratitude that we were able to give him that Bkind moment.

The ramifications are huge. Living a Bkind life impacts our mindset, mental health, physical well-being, family life, colleagues, friends, strangers, and the world around us. Begin with a Bkind practice for yourself. Expand your practice to others in small ways. When you're ready, go big. Bkind in every area of life, and watch the impact you will have.

The Impact of Being Kind to Yourself

Being kind to yourself isn't just about self-care—it has a bigger effect that reaches beyond just you. In this part, let's explore how being kind to myself affects the world around me and makes it a better place for everyone.

Spreading positivity

Every day, our phone's lock screen reminds us to "Uplift one person every day." It's a simple reminder to look for chances to spread positivity and make someone's day a little brighter.

Making a Difference

We make it a point to ask ourselves two questions daily: Did I compliment someone today? Did I help someone with their goals? By actively seeking ways to offer praise and support, we're able to make a positive impact on those around us.

Writing to Inspire Change

Writing this book is another way we are practicing kindness towards ourselves. By sharing our experiences and insights, we hope to encourage others to prioritize self-kindness and spread kindness to others, too. It's not just about expressing ourselves. It's about contributing to a more caring and understanding world.

In short, being kind to ourselves has a ripple effect that can reach far beyond our own lives. By spreading positivity, making a difference in others' lives, and sharing our journey, we're playing a part in creating a world where kindness is valued and practiced by everyone.

> RemindHer: Embrace the quiet power of treating yourself and others with compassion and understanding, knowing that kindness is a strength that transforms lives.

CHAPTER 12

Bbad***

---

*As I face cancer once more, my "Bbada**" necklace and bracelet serve as daily reminders of my strength and resilience. How would a bada** handle this, I often ask myself. This mantra has not only helped me but has also woven itself into the culture of our morning show, enriching relationships around the station, and inspiring both listeners and colleagues alike.*

~CHRISTINE LEE

Chrissy

I often reflect on the wisdom of one of my favorite Peloton instructors. One day as I was sweating my behind off through a Peloton workout, my legs were on fire and about to stage a full-blown rebellion and totally give up on me, she said something I will never forget, I mean she dropped an absolute gem, she said,

"Sometimes you gotta know when to turn shit up so it can go back down." Boom! Exactly what I needed at the exact perfect time. I killed the rest of that workout because of her one sentence. Those words hit me like a shot of espresso at that moment and they've echoed in my head ever since. So simple yet so damn powerful, her mantra has profoundly influenced how I approach challenges and opportunities in my life.

For me, "turning it up" is part of what it means to Bbad***. It's so much more than surviving a spin class, it's like a life hack. It means recognizing those moments when I have the energy, motivation, and mental capacity to push harder, to go all in. It's about seizing those times and giving my all to whatever it is I'm doing. Whether I'm diving into a new project at work, pushing through a killer workout, or dedicating extra time to my personal growth, these are the moments to crank it to eleven. I find comfort in knowing that these high-energy, completely in-the-zone moments are when I can make my most significant strides.

I remember a specific instance when this philosophy played a crucial role. I was working on expanding our jewelry line, and the sheer amount of work felt overwhelming. But instead of letting it paralyze me, I decided I was going to "turn it up." So, I scheduled extra hours, brought our team together for brainstorming sessions, and poured all my creativity into the projects in front of me. The results were phenomenal, not just in terms of business success but also in the euphoric personal satisfaction of knowing I had given it my all.

I realized that in the full-throttle moments, the magic happens because it's when I break through the barriers and surprise myself with what I can achieve. When we turn it up at the right times we're building the momentum that carries us through the together times and making the inevitable downs a bit more bearable.

With that said, Bbad*** isn't just about relentless effort all the time. It's equally important to know when to ease off and allow yourself time to rest and recover your body and mind. After intense periods of hard work, I make it a point to slow down, recharge, and take care of myself for a little while. It's a balance that is uber important and helps me maintain long-term productivity and prevents the dreaded burnout.

She may never know it but the advice from my Peloton instructor that day has become one of my guiding principles in all areas of my life. It reminds me that being a bad*** is about much more than just pushing limits and more about smartly managing my energy and understanding the natural rhythms of my own life. Balancing periods of intense effort with times of rest, we can stay resilient and focused, and ready to tackle anything coming my way. We are not only staying productive, but we genuinely enjoy the journey, every step of it.

Every bad*** knows that life is full of challenges. It is a journey, not a destination. It's about pushing yourself when you need to and slowing down when you need to, it's about personal growth, and enjoying the process along the way. Embrace your inner bad*** and take charge of your destiny. As you read through this chapter, think about how you can apply these principles to your own life. We will explore how to face these challenges head-on with confidence and resilience, transforming obstacles into opportunities for growth.

Being a bad*** is a deeply personal journey. So we'll discuss what it means to Bbad*** defining your own version of bad***ery, breaking away from societal norms and external influences, elevating your future self, and overcoming life's obstacles with confidence, class, and a little sass. WE will provide tips we find so helpful on how to stay true to yourself while embracing your inner bad***. We'll look at the importance of humor and playfulness, and how they significantly contribute to a bad*** attitude. Finally, we will share a few practical exercises to help you reflect on your future self and plan actionable steps towards your goals.

What It Means to Be Bad***

In life, we often come across moments where we need to dig deep to find our inner strength. Bbad*** is about breaking into that inner reservoir and using that power and confidence. It's not about being reckless or overly aggressive, but about being assertive when you need to be, self-assured, and fearless while striving toward your goals.

Our dear friend, you have made it so far. You've got momentum going, you're doing the work, and we hope you are feeling so much better than before you opened this book. And now it is time to turn it up and Bbad***! The bad*** you know you are now for pushing through and the bad*** future self you are becoming along the way.

Defining what it means to be a bad*** is a deeply personal journey. For us, it began with moments of soul-searching and self-reflection. We started by thinking about the times in our life when we felt most powerful and confident. These moments were often tied to overcoming obstacles or achieving something we had worked hard for.

Bbad*** is never about fitting into some predefined mold of what society expects from you. Bbad*** is about creating your own path and living authentically. Society often tries to dictate what success and power look like, but I knew that my version of bad***ery had to align with my values and aspirations, not someone else's expectations. And you should too. Bad*** women stand apart, aren't afraid to be different, and march to the beat of their own drum.

Bbad*** is about taking on the day with confidence, class, and a little sass. Imagine you're on a long car ride, foot on the gas, pumping down the miles, breaking the boundaries. You're up for tackling the challenges of the world, crushing your goals, and whatever else the universe serves you. There may have been times when fear or exhaustion held you back, but now it's time to feel your momentum and keep it going.

Bbad*** can also remind you to channel your adventurous spirit and step out of your comfort zone. Maybe it's taking the opportunity to wakeboard, skiing the Swiss Alps, or taking the plunge and starting your own business. The show we do with 96.5 TIC in Connecticut is Bad*** Women of the Week, and these women are women who take chances, don't take no for an answer, and find a way to do amazing things every single day. They take control of their own lives and write their own story.

This is where you catch your stride. Hard work is simple, not easy, and we promise you that as you start to build more and more momentum, you'll learn how to navigate through your life natu-rally with more confidence. You'll know your body and your mind and your spirit and when they tell you it's time to "turn it up" and when it's time to take a step back. This is the chapter in your life where you begin to understand and stand behind your worth more than ever before.

Defining Your Own Bad***ery

We remember vividly the day our cousin walked into our shared office and confided in our business partner and brother, Lewis, about her overwhelming credit card debt. The weight of it was crushing her, and she felt like she was drowning in a sea of financial obligations. The stress was taking a huge toll on her mentally and emotionally.

During a trip with her mother, she stumbled upon a bracelet inscribed with "Bbad***." The simple piece of jewelry resonated with her deeply. She saw it as a symbol of strength and determination, a reminder that she had the power to overcome her financial struggles. She told her mom, "That's what I need. I need a reminder that I can do this."

Later that day she called us and shared her experience and a suggestion for the next bracelet. "I need a Bbad*** bracelet to help me through this debt." Her words struck a chord. We knew that creating the Bbad*** bracelet would serve as a powerful symbol for her and so many other women facing challenges.

Every time she looked at the bracelet, she felt a surge of motivation. It was a daily reminder of her commitment to becoming debt-free. She knew that getting out of debt required more than just motivation. She worked really hard, made sacrifices, and took it one day at a time. The bracelet served as her beacon of hope, reminding her that she was capable of tackling this financial mountain. Each payment, no matter how small, felt like a victory.

Of course, she had moments of doubt, times when the progress seemed painfully slow, and the temptation to give up was strong. But her perseverance paid off. After months of hard work and dedication, she saw her debt decrease significantly. Each step forward reinforced her belief in her ability to achieve financial freedom. Finally, she reached her goal and became debt-free. I'm sure you can imagine that the sense of empowerment and relief was massive for her.

Inspired by her journey, we decided to incorporate the "Bbad***" bracelet into our brand. It became a symbol of strength, resilience, and the determination to face challenges with a bad***

attitude. Our cousin's story is a testament to the power of self-belief and the incredible things that can be achieved when you refuse to give up.

What You Can Do

Design your future bad*** self. We want you to take a few moments and envision your bad*** self. How does she look? What is she wearing? How does she feel? Confident? Confident in her own mind? In her own body? In her own spirit? What is she doing in her career, family, hobbies, etc.? What is her personal life like? Now, how do you get there? How do you make her a reality?

Take a moment each day to acknowledge the value you bring into the world. Revisit all of our Powerwords, they are yours forever. Read the accomplishments and affirmations you've written down for yourself that remind you of your strength and capabilities. Tell yourself, "I am capable and strong," "I embrace challenges as opportunities for growth," and "I am committed to achieving my goals." believe in yourself.

Remember, Bbad*** means you set clear boundaries and say no to things that don't align with your values or priorities. I know it isn't always easy, especially when it involves disappointing someone you care about, but it is absolutely essential for maintaining your authenticity and focus. Communicate your limits clearly with your friends, family, and coworkers, and stand by them.

Bbad*** is having the courage to be real, raw, and honest. Admitting when you don't know something, asking for help when you know you need it, and openly sharing your fears and struggles with people you trust. There will be times when you doubt your abilities and feel like you don't deserve your success. It's normal to have these feelings sometimes, it's called imposter syndrome and we all get it. But you are learning to recognize these feelings, and making the choice to focus on your achievements and what you are capable of instead.

And if you fail, so what? We all do. Each failure teaches you valuable lessons and brings you closer to your goals. So you jot down what went wrong, adjust your approach, and try again because you are resilient and worth it.

As you take on each day with more confidence, class, and a little sass, we want you to know that you have the power within you to achieve great things. Keep this top of mind: prioritize your self-care, acknowledge your value, and believe there's nothing you can't do, especially when it feels hard. Keep faith in yourself and keep going. Break the boundaries holding you back, tackle the challenges, and embrace every part of yourself. Embrace Bbad*** and show the world what you're capable of.

Elevating Your Future Self

Chrissy

I can remember the first time I truly allowed myself to dream about the future. About ten years ago now, it was a quiet evening, and I found a moment to sit quietly alone. I began by closing my eyes and letting my mind wander, then I started to focus my mind on certain things. Like I focused on my breathing, my chest going up and down with every breath. Then I turned my focus to each part of my body, one at a time, acknowledging and feeling each part head to toe. I was tuned in and present with myself. Now I was ready to envision my future self. I was intentional with what I wanted to envision. I pictured the best version of myself: confident, successful, and genuinely happy. In my vision, I myself stand tall, shoulders back, with a smile that radiates genuine joy. I could see all the amazing accomplishments that lay behind that smile: the goals I had achieved, the challenges I had overcome, and the beautiful life I had built.

Every detail in that vision mattered. I saw the environments I thrived in, the people I surrounded myself with, and the projects I passionately pursued. It wasn't just a fleeting daydream; it was a vivid, powerful exercise that brought my future self to life. Visualization became more than just a mental escape for me, it became a daily habit. Every morning, before the chaos of the day began, I spent a few minutes revisiting my future self. It was a ritual that reminded me of my potential and kept me focused on the steps I needed to take to get there.

I knew exactly what my future self wanted, and I wrote it all down in my journal. Ten years ago, my future self wanted:

- To run a marathon.
- To be debt-free.
- To be a healthier version of myself and set an example for my kids.
- To stop working weekends.
- To hire an assistant.
- Never go on a diet again.

To transform into this future version of myself, I knew I needed to build habits that aligned with my goals. I started small, setting aside time each day for personal development. I committed to practices that nurtured both my mind and body. I read books that inspired me, engaged in regular exercise, and made sure I ate healthily. These weren't just tasks on a to-do list; they were deliberate actions that brought me closer to my vision each day.

Maintaining momentum was key. Progress didn't always come in leaps and bounds. Often, it was the small, consistent steps that made the biggest difference. On days when motivation waned, I had to push myself to take action, no matter how minor it seemed. Each step, no matter how small, compounded over time, leading to significant progress. I kept a journal, documenting my achievements and setbacks, reflecting on them regularly to stay motivated and learn from mistakes

I'm not gonna lie, self-doubt was a familiar antagonist. There were moments when negative thoughts threatened to derail my progress. But instead of letting them control me, I acknowledged them and then shifted my focus to positive affirmations instead. I reminded myself of my strengths and my successes. Everyone starts somewhere, and I learned that growth comes from pushing through the doubt.

Having accountability partners made a tremendous difference too. I surrounded myself with people who supported my vision, like my sister, and trusted friends and mentors who believed in my potential. Sharing my visions, goals, and even setbacks with them and having regular check-ins provided the motivation and accountability I needed to stay on track.

Visual reminders are worth their weight in gold. They became an essential part of my journey. I created a vision board filled with images and quotes that represented my goals. Sticky notes with affirmations adorned my workspace, and my phone's screensaver was a very intentional constant reminder of the life I was working towards. Of course, I have my tattoo and my Powerword bracelets on every day. Visual cues kept my goals top of mind and helped me stay focused on my journey.

I have since run a marathon, my husband and I are debt-free, I have earned my Health Coaching Certificate, and I have completely stopped working weekends. Even when someone requests a meeting on a Saturday, I stay firm, and they are always understanding and willing to reschedule. Maybe one day they will stop working weekends too.

I've certainly caved on the never going on a diet again part, but I am in a much better place than I was before. My focus now is on being strong and healthy, not skinny. Ten years ago I was into the deprivation diet phase. I was sweating my ass off every day to burn all the calories, I was a cardio queen. Now, I focus on feeling satiated when I eat because I'm eating the right amount of protein, fats, and carbs. I'm more focused on healthy muscle and body fat percentage instead of the number on the scale.

By consistently visualizing my future self and taking daily actions toward my goals, I wasn't just dreaming, I was taking action, doing the work, creating the life I wanted. It was a process that required a shit ton of commitment and resilience, but it was incredibly rewarding. So worth it all and embracing this journey transformed me into the bad*** version of myself I envisioned over and over again. Each day brought me closer to that confident, successful, and genuinely happy woman I had first pictured on that quiet evening. With dedication and belief in yourself, absolutely anything is possible.

Confidence

Life is full of unexpected obstacles, and like you, we've faced our fair share of them. We've learned that how you respond to these challenges is what's important, it defines your character. Whenever life throws a curveball, we take a deep breath and face it head-on, armed with our Bbad*** bracelet, confidence, and a positive mindset.

Chrissy

One particular challenge stands out in my memory. It was during that period when work was especially demanding as we expanded the brand. I felt overwhelmed by the sheer volume of tasks to be done. Deadlines loomed, and stress levels were at an all-time high. But instead of surrendering to the pressure, I made the decision to simplify the complexity of it all. I broke down all the overwhelming tasks into smaller, more manageable steps. Then each day, I focused on completing a few smaller tasks, rather than being paralyzed by the size of the entire project.

I also embraced the "turn it up" philosophy, inspired by my Peloton instructor. This mantra, "Sometimes you gotta know when to turn it up so it can go back down," became my guiding principle when I needed to Bbad*** because during those moments of momentum, when I felt energized and capable, I pushed myself harder.

Building resilience also means celebrating all the wins, even the small ones. Every task completed, no matter how minor it may seem, is a step forward. I took time to acknowledge my achievements, which kept me motivated and focused on the goal. Overcoming challenges isn't just about the big wins. Appreciating the journey and the progress made along the way is where the good stuff is.

Facing challenges with confidence, breaking down the complexity, and maintaining resilience, taught me that obstacles are not roadblocks but stepping stones along my path. Each challenge overcome brought me closer to my goals and reinforced my belief in my own strength.

Class

Class comes in many forms. It's about how you present your-self to the world and how you treat others and navigate through life with grace and dignity. Remind yourself what makes you feel good. There's a lot of truth in the saying, "When you look better, you feel better." Taking care of your appearance is not about van-ity; it's about showing up as your best self. When you put effort into self-care, you send a message to yourself and the universe that you value yourself and you are ready to tackle whatever comes your way.

Class isn't just about what you wear; it's reflected in how you interact with others. Being courteous, kind, and respectful in every interaction is a hallmark of true class. Whether you're dealing with a colleague, a friend, or a stranger, treating people with dignity and showing empathy goes a long way. This not only elevates your own sense of self but also inspires others around you to act with the same level of grace.

The way we communicate is a direct reflection of our inner class. This means speaking with intention, listening actively, and choosing words that uplift rather than tear down. It's about being assertive without being aggressive, and clear without being conde-scending. When we speak with class, we set a tone of respect and mutual understanding, which can greatly enhance both personal and professional relationships. One of the true tests of class is how you handle difficult situations.

Do you remain calm and composed, or do you let stress and anger take over? Class is about maintaining your poise even when things don't go your way. It's about finding constructive solutions rather than getting caught up in the drama. By staying centered and responding thoughtfully, you demonstrate strength and integ-rity, making you a true role model for those around you.

Another aspect of class is the commitment to continuous self-improvement. We know that's important to you, because you're reading this book! Keep investing time in learning, expanding your knowledge, and refining your skills. Whether it's reading books, attending workshops, or simply engaging in reflective practices, nurturing your mind and spirit is a sign of class. It shows that you value yourself enough to keep growing and evolving.

The company you keep can also reflect your sense of class. Surround yourself with people who inspire you, challenge you to be better, and who embody the values you hold dear. Being in the presence of like-minded individuals who exhibit class in their actions and attitudes will naturally elevate your own. Moreover, it's about cultivating relationships that are based on mutual respect, support, and understanding.

While class goes far beyond appearances, how you choose to dress and present yourself is an outward expression of your inner confidence. Investing in a wardrobe that makes you feel both comfortable and powerful can have a significant impact on how you carry yourself throughout the day. Choose clothing that reflects your personality and makes you feel like the best version of yourself. Whether it's a tailored suit for a big meeting or a simple yet elegant dress for a casual outing, your style should reflect your inner grace.

Class is also about giving back and showing generosity, not just with material things but with your time, attention, and kindness. Whether it's mentoring someone new in your field, volunteering for a cause you believe in, or simply offering a listening ear to a friend in need, these acts of generosity are a true reflection of your character. It's about leading with your heart and making a positive impact on the lives of others.

Sass: Live in Your Power And Have a Little Fun

Chrissy

There's the time I bought this new ice cream flavor that my kids were really excited to try. To spice things up, I decided to add a little twist. I took a small squirt of mustard and hid it underneath a scoop of ice cream. When I handed the bowl to my kids, they were so excited and their faces lit up. They were completely unsuspecting and innocent, eagerly anticipating the delicious treat.

I was barely able to contain my laughter. Of course, they didn't just take a small bite—they went for a big spoonful. The look of surprise and confusion on their faces was priceless! It was all in good fun, and after the initial shock, we all had a good laugh about it.

My family is full of pranksters. The other day, Rae and I were in the showroom at the jewelry store talking to our dear friend who was very very pregnant and eagerly awaiting her induction scheduled for the following week. She told us she is in "beast mode," as she called it, indulging in all her cravings with the baby coming so soon. She was like "I don't give a shit I'm gonna eat all the croissants and the candy, and the bagels, and the cookies, all of the treats."

Rae keeps a small pretend candy jar tucked away in her purse for times like this. Rae was like, "Oh my gosh, you have to try these, they are so good," as she sprang the candy jar at her. Fully pregnant, her eyes widened as she reached for what she thought was a delicious piece of candy and suddenly the snake flew up at her. I have never seen her jump like that! The initial shock quickly turned to crying about not getting candy and laughing at the same time. She said, "Ooh that was so dirty!" I think all three of us peed our pants from laughing so hard that day. She appreciated the humor.

You see, Bbad*** isn't because you always face challenges with strength. We have to bring joy and laughter into our lives and the lives of those around us too. The candy prank created a memory none of us will ever forget. One we can tell her new baby for years to come.

Maybe you're not a prankster. That's okay because there are endless ways to create joy and laughter in your life! Maybe you like to tell funny stories or jokes to your friends and loved ones. Maybe you enjoy laughing at funny videos on TikTok or YouTube, or maybe you like to watch comedy shows or movies. Maybe you enjoy dancing around the house in your underwear, drawing funny pictures, or playing with your pets. It's endless, and whatever you like to do to bring joy into your life will help you stay connected to your inner child and bring a sense of playfulness into your life.

Creating joyful traditions with family is also a great way to have some fun. Establishing monthly game nights with friends or themed family dinners are things to look forward to! Play stimulates creativity and innovation. When you allow yourself to play, you open up your mind to new possibilities, creativity, and fresh ideas. So whatever it is that brings you joy and makes you laugh, do more of it!

Humor has always been a powerful coping mechanism for us. Even in difficult times, finding humor can be incredibly powerful. It doesn't mean we're ignoring the seriousness of a situation or circumstance, but rather we're finding lightness to help cope. It allows us to see situations from a different perspective and diffuses a lot of tension in challenging moments. We can recall particularly stressful days at work when the showroom floor was chaotic and tensions were high. Pausing for a second to make a joke about the chaos we were all dealing with, and then seeing the smiles, can help alleviate the tension in the room and give everyone a sense of solidarity. It's a little reminder that we're all in this together, and it's all going to be fine.

Laughing at yourself, especially, and finding humor in everyday situations actually helps you stay resilient and grounded. Have fun and enjoy the journey. Fun breaks up the monotony of daily routines and provides a much-needed mental reset. It's such a fun way to connect with others in your life and relieve some stress.

Balancing work and play is something we strive for every day. We schedule time for fun just as we would for important tasks. This balance prevents burnout and keeps us motivated. Play is not a luxury; it's a necessity for a fulfilling life. By incorporating humor and playfulness into your daily routine, you can maintain a positive mindset and build stronger connections with those around you. Embracing your inner child and not being afraid to laugh at yourself is what makes life truly enjoyable and fulfilling.

My Future Bad*** Self

> **Chrissy**

The journey of becoming the woman I want to be is filled with learning, growth, and self-discovery. My future bad*** self embodies confidence in her mind, body, and spirit. She stands on a rock-solid foundation. She's financially secure and has the freedom to make her own schedule.

This journey is never about reaching a specific destination because we are constantly evolving. And right now, I'm working on adjusting the amount of pressure I put on myself. I often equate my personal value with how much I sell at the jewelry store, but my future self knows better. She understands that self-worth isn't tied to sales commissions or financial success. My future self wants me to detach my self-worth from these external metrics entirely.

I'm learning to stop worrying about having the perfect marriage. I have this fear that something will go wrong in my relationship if I'm not the main creative force behind our relationship so I tend to over-plan every date night and manage every detail, and it leaves me exhausted every time. My future self wants me to let go a bit and allow Danny to step up and show up for me too. I have to remind myself that no matter what I will be okay and give him the opportunity to contribute and be present in our relationship, rather than me thinking I need to handle everything. I am opening myself up for mutual support and understanding because relationships work best when both of us put in the work.

I also want to be a realistic role model for my kids. I've realized that constantly striving to set the perfect example isn't sustainable. Relationships are amazing with someone you love, but it doesn't mean it's always easy. Relationships are complex and dynamic, filled with love, arguments, and resolutions. My kids need to see that one person doesn't have to carry the entire burden to make a relationship work. By showing them the reality of balancing effort and letting go, they'll learn that a healthy relationship is about partnership, not perfection.

In my work, I want to focus more on quality rather than quantity. Designing jewelry should be about creating pieces that I'm passionate about, not just producing as much as possible as quickly as possible. I know this shift will allow me to put all my creativity and heart into each design, leading to more meaningful work.

I recognize the importance of finding hobbies outside of work. My future self wants to explore new interests and activities, even though I'm not entirely sure what those might be yet. I am open to discovering new passions that bring me joy and fulfillment beyond the jewelry store.

Lastly, my future self envisions taking four vacations a year, ideally one solo trip, one with my husband, and two with the whole family. I envision these breaks will provide time to recharge, reconnect with my loves, and explore new places, ensuring that life stays balanced, fresh, and energized.

This journey is all about balance, embracing our strengths, and being kind to ourselves through it all. We have to evolve and adjust as we go because our lives, needs, and wants are constantly changing. We're constantly taking on challenges and we want to do them with confidence and allow ourselves to rest and recharge when we need to. The Bbad*** journey is personal and unique to each of us, but it's filled with endless possibilities for growth and fulfillment. So, embrace it with me, with confidence, class, and a little sass, and let's go show the world what we're capable of.

> RemindHer: Own your power and don't be afraid to step into your full potential with beautiful boldness.

CHAPTER 13

Bgrateful/Bblessed

"I bought Bgrateful for my wife, my daughters, and their Grandma. We have a connection through Bgrateful and of course our hearts."

~STEPHEN ALEXANDER

Rae

When my babies were little and I'd hear that cry in the middle of the night I would often smile. I smiled because the level of gratitude I have for being a mom is hard to explain. Getting pregnant was the most difficult challenge I had ever faced and now my home being filled with three healthy children is my biggest blessing. Of course, I have typical mom moments when I feel overwhelmed and tensions running high but those are also the times I feel blessed and am grateful for the noise, the mess, the Legos on the floor, the sibling bickering and all the love at the same time.

At first glance, "Bgrateful" and "Bblessed" might seem like two different things, but they are actually very connected. You can't have one without the other; they are like two sides of the same coin. Gratitude means being thankful for the good things in life. When you are grateful, you notice the blessings around you, no matter how small they are. This makes you feel blessed. On the other hand, when you feel blessed, you naturally feel grateful.

Chrissy

Our sister-in-law Nichole is one of those people who is beautifully intuitive with a heart of gold, and her presence and thoughtfulness perfectly represent B grateful. We have a text exchange and, somehow she always seems to know when we need a bit of encouragement. Thanks Nichole.

In short, being grateful and feeling blessed go hand in hand. When you are grateful, you see more blessings in your life; when you see more blessings, you feel more grateful. You need to be grateful to feel blessed, and feeling blessed makes you grateful.

In a world full of trouble and hardship, it may be difficult at times to feel grateful and blessed, but with a little focus and skill, it can become second nature. Sometimes, we feel impatient to receive the blessings we've been going for, instead of focusing on what we have already.

I didn't really understand the phrase "It's not the time" until I felt naturally drawn to something without forcing it. Before, I always rushed into things instead of letting life flow. This lesson became clear during a meeting with a client who had recently lost her wife.

She came to me wanting to have me restyle her wedding rings into a different piece of jewelry because she thought she didn't need them anymore. I immediately sensed that she was trying to speed through her grief. I told her that she might be trying to skip the natural grieving process, and encouraged her to stop and think about the happy memories she shared with her spouse and spend time being grateful for them before making a decision about the wedding rings.

I showed her the words, "It's not the time." These words remind us to be patient and let life unfold naturally, especially during tough times. It's important to give yourself the time you need to fully experience and process each moment, even the hard ones. This helps with deeper healing and a better appreciation of life's journey.

Timing is everything. You never know what life will bring or what unexpected blessings may be in store. By keeping a Bgrateful attitude, you are ready for those blessings when the timing is right. I grew deep into my understanding of this with the birth of my two miracle babies.

When a doctor told me I would probably never get pregnant, I would never have believed that I'd someday have two healthy babies. This incredible journey has changed my life and my beliefs.

Growing up Catholic, I learned a lot about faith and prayer. However, there was a time when I felt disconnected from my faith (I'll tell you that story soon). Over the years, I stopped praying and drifted away from those teachings.

Everything changed when I found out I was pregnant with my second baby. The news was so overwhelming that it brought me to my knees. At that moment, I remembered the power of prayer. Having my two miracle babies rekindled my faith. It brought me back to praying, something I had forgotten for a long time.

These unexpected blessings taught me that life can surprise us in amazing ways and that faith, even when it seems lost, can come back in moments of pure joy. We never know what is around the next corner. Life will bring challenges and hardships. Keeping a Bgrateful / Bblessed attitude keeps us looking for the good in life and facing the difficulties with spiritual power.

A few years later, in 2019, we decided to go to the Women's Rise Conference with Rachel Hollis. At the time, we were thinking about rebranding our company, The Power to B. It was the two of us and one of our close friends. The experience was powerful for both of us, but in different ways.

My Spiritual Journey: The Importance of Prayer

> ### Chrissy

I had a lot of mom guilt about going to the conference but convinced myself it was necessary. After a long day, I felt exhausted and went back to the hotel room while they went for manicures and pedicures. In the quiet of the room, I felt the need to pray for clarity and guidance. It was one of those unexplainable yet powerful moments. It was this moment that reaffirmed the importance of prayer in my life. Now, it's an almost daily practice for me.

Prayer is a foundational element of a Bgrateful/Bblessed life. My faith journey has been bumpy at times, but through it all, I have found that prayer is a sustaining power.

I got married in the Catholic Church to please my family and because I never thought of another option. Saying no never even occurred to me. Years later, I decided that if something wasn't a "heck yes," it was a "no." This change in my thinking led me to question my relationship with religion when my children were born.

I had always planned for my sister to be godmother to our babies. However, she married a wonderful man who happens to be Jewish and didn't get married in the church, which meant she couldn't fulfill that role, according to our priest. When the priest who married me called to talk about baptizing our daughter, Scarlet, I learned my sister couldn't be her godmother. I couldn't imagine anyone else having that role. Then, there were the implications of what might happen if my child went unbaptized. The priest talked about original sin and purgatory. I decided then and there that fear-based religious teachings had no place in my life.

I'm not here to criticize the Catholic religion. There are still traditions I love and keep. Yet, I believe you can create your own spiritual path. Even in the years when I stopped praying between the birth of my two children, I didn't lose my need for spiritual connection and guidance.

Despite doctors telling me I'd never get pregnant again, a few years later, I felt nauseous one night while my husband, Danny, was on a work trip. I took several pregnancy tests, and all were positive. Overwhelmed, I fell to my knees, saying, "Thank you, thank you, thank you." I cried and found myself wrapped in a prayer of gratitude. Then, I called my sister.

"Rae, I think I'm pregnant," I whispered.

"Did you take a test?"

"I took a whole box of them. They're all positive."

"Well, then, it's safe to say you're probably pregnant. Call Danny," she replied.

I did just that, and through the following years, I found my way back to prayer as an outlet for uncertainty, but also as a way to express gratitude.

Prayer, at its core, is about connecting with the deepest part of your mind and consciousness. It helps me find direction and feel aligned with my path. That's why I recommend it as a part of tapping into your own power. When you ask for guidance and stay open to possibilities, you'll feel called and guided in the right direction.

Spirituality Is Different from Religion

Rae

Chrissy and I were raised Catholic. I did the communion, the confirmation, and Sunday school. Looking back, I don't know why I did it. I remember sitting there and thinking, "I want to question that. Should I question that?" I had a lot of doubt on the beliefs that I was taught I was supposed to have. You can go to church, but do bad things and still be a good Christian, be forgiven, and go to heaven. That didn't make sense to me.

I married into an interfaith family. My husband was raised Jewish, and as our relationship progressed, I learned a lot about how he was raised in his religion. Although to me, it kind of seemed like he was keeping the traditions because his family had such a rich Jewish culture, and there was some pride in continuing those traditions rather than whole heartedly aligning with his beliefs.

My marriage isn't acknowledged in the Catholic church because I married a Jewish man and we had an interfaith ceremony. I could have had it acknowledge in the Catholic religion, after all, that how I was raised but I chose not to because having a Catholic priest bless my marriage is not what was going to make my marriage "real."

Not being able to be my sister's daughter's godmother was a final push to make it clear to me that organized religion wasn't for me. I was going to have my own faith, my own way. My husband

and I started talking about what our family would do with regard to religion. We decided that we have our own spirituality that is part of us, and we want to teach our children to be good humans, with good morals and to do good in the world without the rigidity and the rules of structured religion.

I have faith and spirituality, I believe in being a good human, kindness, love, and karma, I know in my soul that the universe has my back. I practice gratitude, I meditate, and I still pray (in my own way).

Making It Happen

One of the easiest things you can do to boost your mood and elevate your mind, body, and spirit is to focus on gratitude. Take a moment to think about what you're thankful for, say it out loud, or write it down. Even on tough days, recognizing the good things in your life can make a big difference.

Feeling grateful isn't always easy. Sometimes, you might feel stuck and find it hard to feel happy or excited. It's like your joy is hidden away, and gratitude is the tool that helps you find it again. That's why saying it out loud or writing it down is so crucial. Don't approach your Bgrateful/Bblessed life with a casual attitude. Live it intentionally. That's the only way to get through all the noise of life.

Psychologists call this selective attention. Our brains are processing countless activities every second. Everything from taking our next breath to hearing the distant car horn is processed through our brains. Most of it we never even notice. It's not part of our conscious experience.

The things our brains will notice are the things that will bring us physical or emotional harm. We see the bad stuff so that we can avoid them or at least try to avoid them next time. Since good things aren't going to harm us, the blessings of life can be absorbed into the constant noise and endless activity that our brains process every day.

To live a Bgrateful/Bblessed life, we must not let our blessings fade away. Instead, we need to pay attention to them on purpose. There are two easy ways to do this effectively.

The first is to say it out loud. When we speak about what we're thankful for, it's like a form of prayer. It helps us focus on our blessings and gives them importance in our lives.

The second is to write it down. Taking the time to jot down what we're grateful for makes us really think about it. It keeps our minds on gratitude so that our attention isn't getting lost in the busyness of life.

Talking to yourself out loud can be surprisingly effective. This morning, while I was getting ready, I paused and reminded myself to speak up. I asked, "What do I want to do today?" Then, I reassured myself, saying, "Take it easy; you've already done your workout, got some rest, and you're ready for this meeting." Saying it out loud made me feel more confident.

You can also use self-talk to express your desires or seek guidance. For instance, you might say, "I'd like to pray for some clarity and guidance for [insert situation]." It's okay to admit when you're feeling overwhelmed or unsure and ask for a sign to help you decide. Speaking it aloud can help clear your mind and make it easier to receive guidance or insight.

Remember the principles we learned in Bopen. Signs are all around us. Our task is to slow down and pay attention enough to see them. Learn to ask for signs and then be playful and curious enough to look for them throughout your day. Look for the blessing you expect and pay attention to the wonderful surprises that you never even thought to ask for. Then, when you receive the sign or blessing you've been looking for, take action.

Show gratitude and live into that blessing. This becomes part of living Blimitless. In the chapter where we explored Blimitless, we learned to put aside limiting beliefs and keep dreaming. The same principles come into play here as well. As we are blessed with our dreams coming into reality, we express our gratitude, knowing there is no limit to the blessing we can receive. There's no reason to live in doubt. Celebrate the blessings and look for the next wave of good things to come. There will be plenty of hardships in life, but there is no reason to let these put limits on us. Keep dreaming, find the blessings, and express your gratitude.

In a world where problems can feel overwhelming, it's easy to forget about the good things, big or small, that happen every day. That's where Bgrateful comes in. It's about finding thankfulness in any moment, big and small.

When life gets tough, being grateful might not fix everything, but it can help us focus on something positive instead of just our problems. It's like taking a breather from the stress of the moment and setting our minds on the life we want our future selves to experience.

"I'm going to make choices with her in mind" means thinking about our future selves and making decisions that will bene-fit them. Even on tough days or when things are going well, it's important to remember what we're thankful for.

This is a skill that seems to be tough to find today. It's as if our society has forgotten the simple act of saying 'thank you.' Gratitude isn't just a nice feeling—it's like a boost that keeps us going. It helps us move forward and keeps us on track for a better tomorrow.

So, try to be more grateful, not just when things are going great, but all the time. It's a reminder to appreciate what we have and to spread a little kindness wherever we go.

Finding Your Way

Part of finding the blessing you want in your life is being on the path that is right for you. When you are moving in the right direction, your blessings are lying along the way. That is why it is vital that we constantly keep ourselves in alignment by praying for clarity and guidance.

In life, we often come to points where we have to make big decisions. It's like standing at a crossroads, not sure which way to go. That's when we need clarity and guidance, a clear idea of what to do next.

A great practice is to seek clarity and guidance every day. Make it a habit as you are driving to work. Take a moment to pray for guidance. It's a quiet time; there's nothing in the car except the sounds of traffic. Ask for help in figuring out the right path to take in all of the decisions you will make that day.

It doesn't need to be elaborate. Simple works just fine. "I pray for clarity and guidance" is an easy mantra that gets to the point. Don't be surprised in that moment if you hear something inside you that tells them what to do.

Yet, it's not just about asking for help; it's also about being thankful for the help we've already received. It's about recognizing the signs that have shown us where to go, even when it was hard to see.

With a Bgrateful attitude in our hearts, we promise to try our best to follow the path we've been shown. We know there will be bumps along the way, but we trust that we'll be okay because we have guidance. When we start each new day this way, we live in alignment and believe that we'll find our way, no matter what.

It's also important to remember that Bblessed means not being afraid to ask for the good things you want or need. It's perfectly fine to speak up and say what you want and need, anytime.

In life, we're often told to be thankful for what we have, and that's important, but it's also okay to ask for more. Whether it's asking for help when things are tough, looking for chances to grow, or just saying what you want, don't be afraid to ask for blessings.

Speak up and ask for the good things you deserve. Sometimes, simply asking is the first step to getting what you want. Expect that it will happen, and when it does, Bgrateful.

Do This Today

If you find the idea of being grateful a bit weird, strange, or awkward, here's a simple way to start: say thank you. It's a small thing, but it means a lot. It lays the groundwork for your Bgrateful/Bblessed life, and you can live it out through a simple three-step process.

Thank others.

Thank yourself.

Thank your spirit leader, whoever that may be, the universe, or what you define as your higher power.

Start by thanking someone who's done something nice for you, even if it's just holding a door or pouring you a cup of coffee. You can't do this too much. Imagine if we all made a habit of noticing and appreciating the little acts of kindness around us— how it could change everything.

It begins with speaking these words to others, then grows into a habit of being kind to yourself. When you do something good, like finishing your workout or making yourself a nice meal, take a moment to thank yourself. Acknowledge your efforts and celebrate your accomplishments, no matter how small they may seem.

Then, don't forget to thank your higher power. Whatever you believe in, whether it's God, the universe, or something else, take a moment to express your gratitude. This isn't just for religious folks—it's for everyone who is conscious of the little surprises, the beautiful moments, and unexpected plot twists that worked out in our favor. It's about recognizing the good things in your life and feeling thankful for them.

Remember, both good days and bad days are opportunities for growth. Instead of feeling like life is happening to you, think of it as happening for you. You are working together with your higher power and those around you to create your experiences of life. Tough times will come along, but they are teaching you something important. So, embrace the challenges and trust that they're leading you toward something better.

Your Future Self Is Counting On You

Bgrateful/Bblessed is like any other skill, the more you practice, the better you get. It's a beautiful cycle of noticing the blessings and expressing gratitude, which leads to more blessings, which leads to more gratitude. Start today with the simple words "thank you" and keep expanding from there. Learn to ask for the blessing you want. Learn to see the blessings even in the tough times. Allow the Bgrateful/Bblessed cycle to grow to the point you can find the joy you've always wanted.

How is all this possible? Believing is crucial for any kind of change. If you don't think you can do it or if you're not honest about what's holding you back, nothing will really change. It's about trusting that the person you want to become in the future is real and counting on you to make it happen.

It might sound strange, but believing in your future self can make a big difference. The tricky part is listening to that future version of yourself. You're probably more used to listening to the doubts and fears of your past self. It's an easier voice to hear, but your past self will only hold you back into what you were. To grow, you need to learn to pay attention to what your future self is saying. She knows what you need to do to become her.

So, believe in yourself and your future. Listen to what your future self is telling you because she knows the way forward. Find that clarity and guidance to live your Bgrateful/Bblessed life. With belief and a willingness to listen, you can become that future self you dream of being.

RemindHer: Recognize the blessings in your life every day, no matter how big or small.

CHAPTER 14

Bpresent

"Keep your head where your feet are. Slow down and appreciate the simple things in life."

~ALISA PICERNO

Rae

One of the most impactful lessons I took away from the RISE conference was to be where your feet are, a simple yet powerful phrase. There's a time and place to reflect and plan, but not every minute of every day. Spending too much time in the past or future is harmful to both your mind and body."

I teach this concept to my kids and strive to live by it myself. In our daily lives, we're constantly pulled in different directions—by phones, work, emails, kids, TV, social media, and more. To combat this, my husband and I make it a point to sit down each week, look at our calendar, and plan for the days ahead. This helps us identify moments where we need to be prepared, allowing us to truly "be where our feet are" during the week. By setting aside time for planning, we reduce the need to worry about what might happen and can focus on the present.

This lesson is especially important for my older daughter, who often worries about the future and what comes next. I frequently remind her to stay present, so she doesn't miss out on what's happening right now. For example, she was recently feeling anxious about an end-of-year test at school. I questioned why they were discussing it so far in advance with children who are only seven years old. In moments like these, I guide her back to the present, encouraging her to focus on today rather than what might happen in the future. I remind her to be where her feet are.

Chrissy

There was a time not long ago when work consumed every aspect of my life. We were renovating the jewelry store, building The Power to B brand, and scaling Baribault Jewelers to the next level all at the same time. I was so busy that Danny and the kids would come to the store for dinners because I was literally always there. There was so much going on and I was constantly feeling anxious, everything felt hard and unbalanced.

One evening, I found myself on my closet floor (the same floor where Danny once helped me look for a lost tampon—that floor has been through it), crying—overwhelmed and completely exhausted. Honestly, being a doer is both a blessing and a burden. I could always get it all done, but I always felt rushed and always missing out on the present moments. Life felt like it was on fast-forward, with everything flying by in a blur. I was in the middle of it but I was missing it all.

That moment on the therapeutic closet floor was another turning point for me. Through my total meltdown, I realized I was not being truly present for any of the moments in my life. I felt it deeply in my core, I needed to slow down and start being intentional about my time and what I do with it. I needed to take my life back.

Life is a precious gift, and we only get one short one. Live it with intention, and fill it with power, joy, and light. Be intentional in the things you do. Make conscious choices that align with your values and goals. Remember to focus on what truly matters and let go of what doesn't. And please have a lot of fun along the way.

Sometimes that's easier said than done, I know. But it's important to know that Bpresent isn't only for the good days. Think of Bpresent as a tool that supports you through all the days, good, bad, and all the days in between. When you practice Bpresent, you build resilience that helps you navigate life's challenges gracefully.

There's a silly misconception that we need to do everything and be happy about it to be successful. However, trying to juggle everything at once will lead to burnout and ironically a lack of fulfillment. The goal is to prioritize and focus on what's most important at any given moment. Breaking it all down into manageable chunks will allow us to give your best to each task and experience without feeling overwhelmed.

What Is Bpresent?

Bpresent is fully being in whatever moment you are in at the time. It's to pause and live in the moment that is actually happening in front of you. It's real-life living. To me, Bpresent means:

Loving fully, opening your heart to the people around you, showing them compassion and understanding. It's being there for others and so importantly, being there for yourself. It's creating meaningful connections that genuinely enrich your life.

Loving fully involves:

- **Active Listening:** Pay full attention when someone is speaking to you. Put away distractions and focus on the person in front of you. This not only shows respect but also deepens your connection.

- **Empathy and Compassion:** Try to understand others' perspectives and feelings. Show compassion in your actions and your words and offer support and kindness whenever you can.

- **Self-Love:** Loving fully starts with loving yourself. Take time for self-care, acknowledge your strengths, and be gentle with yourself. When you are full of love for yourself, you can give love more freely to others.

Laugh freely because laughter is medicine, and it is a powerful way to Bpresent with your people. Laughter brings joy and lightens and lifts everyone's spirit. Don't ever hold back your laughter—embrace it fully and let it fill your moments with happiness.

Embracing Laughter Means . . .

- **Finding Humor in Everyday Life:** Look for opportunities to laugh, whether it's watching a funny movie, sharing jokes with friends, or finding the humor in life's absurdities.

- **Being Playful:** Allow yourself to be silly and playful. Engage in activities that make you laugh and bring out your inner child.

- **Sharing Laughter:** Laughter is contagious. Share it with others to create a positive and uplifting environment.

When you laugh with others, you strengthen your bonds and create lasting memories.

- **Living in the Moment** and keeping your head where your feet are so you can notice the pleasure around you.

Embrace Living in the Moment

- **Don't Dwell on the Past or Worry about the Future:** The past is gone, and the future is uncertain and what you have in the moment is real. It's up to you to make the most of it.
- **Mindfulness Practices:** Engage in mindfulness activities such as meditation, deep breathing, or mindful walking. These practices help you stay grounded and focused on the present.
- **Gratitude:** Practice gratitude by acknowledging and appreciating the good things in your life right now. Keeping a gratitude journal can help you stay focused on the present and cultivate a positive mindset.
- **Presence in Daily Activities:** Be fully engaged in whatever you are doing. Whether it's eating, working, or spending time with loved ones, focus on the activity at hand without distractions.

Bpresent for All the Days

Chrissy

The other night we threw a surprise party for my sister. I wore my Bpresent bracelet because I wanted the reminder to let everything else go and be fully present in this moment. After all, It took a lot of effort to gather all her favorite women in one room and it was so hard to keep it a secret from Rae. These gatherings don't happen often, so I wanted to make sure to soak it all in. I fully enjoyed every interaction. I ate my food slowly, savoring its flavors. We all sat around the table talking about our husbands, kids, life, you know how it is when you get together with the girls. I laughed so hard and had so much fun that night that I was even grateful for peeing my pants a little. It felt so good to be present with these beautiful women. I love to laugh from my core and to fully be in the moment.

But When Bpresent Is Hard

We have talked about how Bpresent lets you experience a state of calm and peace. When you focus on the here and now, you can enjoy the moment and you won't be stressing about all the other shit. Even stupid tasks like doing the dishes (I hate doing dishes), can be opportunities to practice mindfulness and find satisfaction in the presence of the task. When I'm present and doing the dishes I just remind myself it's an easy task and I'll feel way better when it's done. If nothing else, and the shit hits the fan you get to say "I did the dishes today." and everything else is a bonus.

Being present doesn't always feel great, especially during tough times (I'm talking tougher than dishes). When we're really struggling in a really hard moment in life, feeling full of anxiety and full of worry and uncertainty, we have to stop, take a step back, and ask ourselves what we need to do for ourselves in this dreadful moment. Say it out loud, "What is it that I need right now?" Then we meet that need halfway. You don't have to do it all right now and be perfect about it. But you can meet it halfway. For example, if you are feeling overwhelmed and completely exhausted and what you need is an hour or ten of sleep but you only have ten minutes until you have to do your next task, use that ten minutes to wrap yourself in a weighted blanket and let yourself rest. It doesn't matter how big or small the action is, what matters is that you use your tools and do something that will help you out of the slump. You might be surprised by what you uncover in the process.

Sometimes our anxiety takes over and everything feels huge, like every task looks like a hurdle you worry is too high for you to leap over. When you feel like you're drowning in life and don't know if you can make it another step, we want you to remember this little slice of scientific evidence about worry. Research shows that most of our worries are actually unfounded. How can that be? It sure doesn't feel that way, right? Well, according to a study by LaFreniere and Newman (2019), where the average person reported three or four testable worries per day, the result was surprising.[9] They found that 91 percent of worries the participants reported were actually false alarms. And of the remaining nine percent, the outcomes were better than expected about a third of the time. For about one in four participants, none of their worries materialize at all.

Now if I really think about this, it makes so much sense. How many times have you laid awake worried about how whatever it is that has to be done tomorrow will turn out? You lay there and envision the most horrific outcomes possible and you are sure the outcome will be exactly how you think it will. Then when tomorrow comes and you do the thing, it turns out that all that worry was a huge waste of precious sleep time. Everything turned out fine and you will live to see another day. I would argue that these study results seem pretty spot on and are a powerful reminder

---

9   LaFreniere, Lucas S., and Michelle G. Newman. "Exposing Worry's Deceit: Percentage of Untrue Worries in Generalized Anxiety Disorder Treatment." *Behavior Therapy* 51, no. 3 (2020): 413–23. https://doi.org/10.1016/j. beth.2019.07.003.

about the importance of staying present and not letting your anxieties and worries consume you.

Grounding and Presence

Being present in the moment is a concept that many of us struggle with, especially in the whirlwind of modern life. Whether we're juggling responsibilities, facing stressors, or simply trying to find peace in the chaos, staying grounded in the present can feel elusive. But what does it really mean to Bpresent?

Visual Reminders: The Power of Tangibility

We interviewed Licensed professional counselor, Nuriye Rumeli to learn about how visual reminders can help. She shared that the use of visual reminders, like bracelets or other tangible items, is not just about aesthetics—it's about creating anchors that keep us tethered to the present moment. Nuriye explains, "Visual reminders like bracelets, jewelry, pictures, religious or spiritual items become tangible visual anchors in the present, especially important when the mind wanders or we feel overwhelmed. They bring us back to the present and engage our senses in a physical way to keep us in the here and now."

This insight is vital because we can't always rely on what we've learned in therapy or self-help books to carry us through every challenge. "When we're calm and having a good day, it's easy to think positively, breathe, and remember those affirmations. But in moments of distress, when we lack the strength or energy to keep our logical brain online, these tangible reminders become crucial," she adds.

Grounding Exercises: A Path Back to Neutral

One of the challenges of being present is dealing with the highs and lows of our emotional states. In our conversation, Nuriye described grounding exercises as essential tools for regaining balance. "When you're spiraling upwards—feeling anxious, breathing rapidly—or spiraling downwards—feeling frozen and unable to move—grounding exercises help bring you back to a neutral state. They allow you to rest, digest, and connect to the present moment."

Grounding is not about eliminating distress; rather, it's about recognizing that you're okay in the present moment, and that all the emotions you experience are temporary. "They keep you in the here and now," Nuriye said in our interview.

The Science Behind Grounding

Physiologically, grounding exercises help reduce anxiety and stress by training the body to access a grounded state even in moments of calm. Nuriye likens this practice to training for a marathon: "You have to practice grounding exercises when you're not stressed, so that when you do face stress, your body knows how to return to that grounded state."

Before starting a grounding exercise, Nuriye advises checking in with your environment. "Is this a safe space to do a grounding exercise? Notice the room you're in, the noise level. If there are no threats, you're more likely to have a successful grounding experience. Connect with the feeling of being physically safe before you start."

Favorite Grounding Techniques

Nuriye shares some of her favorite grounding exercises, emphasizing that there's no one-size-fits-all approach. "Check in with yourself—what's happening? Do you need to calm down, or do you need to bring yourself up from a down place?"

She often imagines a spiral: "Is it spinning up or spinning down? I use my breathing to try to turn the spiral in the other direction." For those who struggle to visualize, looking at a picture of a spiral can be helpful.

Other techniques she recommends include:

- **54321 Method:** Identify five things you can see, four things you can touch, three things you can hear, two things you can smell, and one thing you can taste.
- **Walking on Tippy Toes:** This triggers the survival instinct, pulling you out of the flight, fight, or freeze response.
- **Standing on One Leg:** Switch between legs to engage your body and mind.
- Smelling essential oils: A necklace infused with essential oils can be a discreet way to ground yourself.
- **Chewing Gum or Candy:** The act of chewing can also help ground you.

"Play around and see what works for you. There is no right or wrong," Nuriye encourages.

Integrating Grounding Into Daily Life

Grounding exercises can be tailored to fit your unique needs and preferences. Nuriye advises practicing these techniques in a calm environment to find what works best. "Have some techniques that are more obvious and some that are less so, so you can access that grounded space wherever you need to."

She also addresses common challenges people face when incorporating grounding exercises into their routine. "If people struggle with grounding, it's usually because they don't believe it works or they're not matching the exercise to the moment. For instance, if you're highly anxious and feeling fidgety, you may need to go for a walk or stretch. If you're frozen, you may need faster breathing."

Grounding As Part of a Broader Mental Health Strategy

Grounding exercises are a key component of a broader mental health strategy that includes therapy, mindfulness, and self-care. "These practices help us manage high-stress situations, trauma flashbacks, and triggers. But they can also be part of our day-to-day self-care, teaching us to come back into our bodies and giving ourselves the break and space we need," Nuriye explained in our interview.

For those who feel they don't have the time for grounding, she offered a practical perspective: "Grounding exercises don't have to take twenty minutes. You can do them by looking at your charm bracelet or watch, or taking a walk to the restroom. Even thirty seconds can make a difference."

Real-Life Applications and Advice for Beginners

Grounding exercises can be combined with other therapeutic techniques to enhance their effectiveness. In real-life scenarios, they can be particularly helpful in managing anxiety during meetings, calming nerves before public speaking, or simply reconnecting with the present moment during a hectic day.

Nuriye's advice for those new to grounding exercises or feeling skeptical about their effectiveness is simple: "You don't need to carve out extra time. Incorporate grounding into your daily routines—while brushing your teeth, drinking your morning coffee, or making the kids' lunches. Use these moments to come into the present and teach your brain how good it feels to regulate."

As you begin to practice these techniques, remember that, like driving, it may be difficult at first. But with practice, it becomes automatic, and you'll find yourself naturally reaching for these tools when you need them most. If you want more from Nuriye, you can find her at realmsoflifecounseling.com.

Chrissy

Somedays when I'm at one of the kids soccer, basketball, or baseball games I really have to work sometimes to put my phone down because being present and watching their games isn't something I can get back to later. It's a moment in their lives that's actually happening and it's important to them. If you played sports as a kid you have a memory of looking for your parents in the stands. If your kid looks up and sees you on your phone, how would you feel about that? When attending your child's activities, put away your phone and be fully present. Anything else can wait.

Simplifying Life

Chrissy

One Sunday night, Danny was called into work because there had been a shooting. He left in a hurry and wasn't gone for more than five seconds when Scarlet came down with a fever. Kash had injured his ankle during a soccer game earlier. And I was in the middle of making dinner. So I've got ice on Kash's ankle, I'm trying to get Scarlet in the shower, and trying to make sure dinner doesn't burn. Danny was gone and it was a lot to deal with.

Finally, at the end of the night, I get Scarlet in bed. Normally, I would have felt the need to do everything perfectly, including washing the dishes immediately after dinner. But that night, I was done. I had had enough and I was not washing the damn dishes.

Mondays are supposed to be my self-care days, but instead, I woke up to a pile of dishes and a mountain of laundry. I know this is all normal life stuff but this day, it felt like I was in an overwhelming pile of life. Ugh, where do I start? In these moments when life is overwhelming it is easy to slip into negativity and say things like, "I have to do all these dishes, I hate dishes, this is going to take forever and it's the last thing I want to do right now." But because of everything I have learned, the tools I keep in my belt, and my Powerwords, I didn't let myself go negative. Instead, I started a list with the most important thing and I started doing one and I kept doing another one thing and another one at a time until I was done. And guess what, when I was done, it was all fine and I still got my self-care Monday afternoon.

My point is to prioritize tasks when life feels overwhelming because simplifying your tasks can help you regain control. I like to make a list of everything I need to do and categorize them by importance and urgency. Then I highlight the three most important tasks and I focus on completing those first. Or maybe you rather start by checking off five small, easy tasks. What's important is doing it the way that feels good to you. There is no right or wrong way in any of this.

Don't stop at prioritizing your personal to-do list. Look for ways to streamline your daily activities at work to reduce your stress and actually increase efficiency. Ask yourself what you can do to simplify your tasks at work. If you are feeling overwhelmed, try having a talk with your boss about prioritizing tasks. Or If someone adds something to your already overflowing plate, ask for a clear deadline. It may feel like the task needs to be done right away but often, the urgency is not as immediate as it seems.

If the task must be done quickly, all they really want is a timeline from you right now. Maybe you can't get to it until tomorrow so you negotiate a realistic timeline that allows you to manage your workload effectively.

Or maybe you are your own boss. Are you overwhelmed by your to-do list because you literally do everything for your business? Are there things you do that you could be delegating to someone else because you don't realistically have time to do your passion work (the reason you started your business in the first place) and all the other stuff you have to do to keep the business going? You worry and stress day and night about how you will get it all done let alone make some real money and grow. If this sounds familiar like so many of my entrepreneur friends, you need to find a "who, not how." Hire people to help you. Letting go of the reins even a little bit in your business is hard, I know, but you will have to do it if you want to keep and grow your business and actually have a personal life too. You can start slow with an assistant who works five hours a week. Like anything else uncomfortable at first, you will soon see and love the benefits.

Give Yourself Grace

> **Rae**

This morning my seven year old daughter, Eva was excited to wake up and write in her daily journal just like me. She was so focused on this. Her sentences were great, her spelling was on point, her handwriting was the best she'd done. She called for me with excitement to share her journal entry.

At the same time my four-year-old was also calling for me. I came up the stairs to say good morning to the girls (there rooms are next to one another) when my four year old began to tell me, "I had an accident when I was sleeping last night, but don't worry mommy, it was a very small accident... very, very small."

This meant she peed the bed—all of the bed. The comforter, blankets, sheets, mattress protector, and even the pillows. I began getting her cleaned up, changing sheets, cleaning the mattress, getting her dressed, brushing teeth, and getting everyone ready for school.

I turned to Eva, now standing at the door journal entry in hands, "I am so excited to read your journal, but I want to read it when I can pay attention to all the thoughtful words you wrote. Would you mind if we wait until I'm done getting your siblings ready for the day and then I will be there, ready to focus and excited to read your journal?"

She responded simply and with excitement "Okay Mom!"

I could have said, "I can't, not now! I'm doing all the things."

But I didn't. That same morning, I had written in my journal I was going to be thoughtful in my words and responses today, patient and kind and give my family the love I wanted to receive in return. I stayed true to my daily affirmation, I gave myself grace to not have to attend to everyone's needs all at once and knew that small moment was a win.

When Bpresent Is Hard: Journal for Reflection

We have to Bhonest about what we need to feel like the best version of ourselves at any moment. Ask yourself what your future self would want you to do now. Reflection helps prioritize self-care and Bpresent.

- Journaling is a powerful tool for processing emotions and clearing your mind. When you write down your worries, fears, and frustrations, you create space in your brain for more positive and productive thoughts. Journaling helps gain perspective on your problems and often reveals solutions that weren't apparent before. I like to try different journaling techniques so here are some of my favorites:

- **Brain Dump:** Take a few minutes each day to write down everything that's on your mind. Don't worry about grammar or structure, just get it all out of your head and onto the paper.
- **Angry Write:** If you're feeling particularly frustrated or angry, let it out on the paper. Write as if no one will ever see it. Scribble, use harsh words and rip through the paper if you feel like it. The release can be incredibly cathartic.
- **List-Making:** when you find yourself spinning on all the things you have to do, worry about missing a swim lesson sign-up, etc. just writing the list of to-dos can help get them out of your brain so you can focus on being present. This can be on paper, a voice memo, a text from your husband, etc.

After you're done writing, If you feel so inclined, you can tear up or burn the pages as a symbolic act of letting go. This can provide a sense of closure and relief of those nasty feelings.

Practical Applications for Bpresent

At any moment, you can give yourself the gift of Bpresent. It's a simple act that will change your life. You will feel richer and like your life has more meaning. Living in the moment allows you to experience joy, manage stress, and build stronger connections with the people around you. We know we make it sound easier than it actually is sometimes, so we put together some ideas to help you clear your mind and practice Bpresent.

- **Driving Time:** Driving is often seen as a mundane task, but it can be an opportunity for empowerment. Instead of zoning out, consider using this time to listen to audiobooks or podcasts that inspire and educate you. Transform your commute into a productive and enriching experience.
- **Daily Tasks:** We realized that being present doesn't mean pretending to love every task. It means accepting the task as it is and focusing on the benefits of completing it. Daily chores like doing the dishes can feel stupid, but they can offer a chance to practice being present. Instead of rushing through them, focus on the process and the satisfaction of completing the task. Remind yourself that these small tasks contribute to your overall well-being.
- **Handling Overwhelm:** When life feels overwhelming, it's essential to recognize the signs—fast breathing and a racing mind. Implement grounding exercises to bring yourself back to the present. Simple actions like walking on your tiptoes or using clock visualization can help turn off the fight-or-flight response and restore your calm.
- **RemindHer:** From the girl who has a permanent tattoo "RemindHer" as a reminder to set the reminders we need to see because when life gets hard we almost always forget to set the visual reminders in place that we need. Every day we choose one of our Powerword bracelets to wear as a reminder. You don't have to ink your body or buy all the bracelets to use as reminders, although you can if you want. You can find other ways to set reminders for yourself throughout the day. We all carry cell phones everywhere we go, maybe you set reminders on your alarm to go off throughout your day. Customize your alarm with phrases or Powerwords that pop up for you as the alarm rings.

- **Mindful Eating:** This can be another practice of mindfulness. Instead of rushing through meals, take the time to savor each bite. Pay attention to the flavors, textures, and aromas of your food. This not only enhances your eating experience but also helps you to slow down and appreciate the moment.
- **Nature Walks:** Spending time in nature alone or with a friend or loved one is a great way to ground yourself and Bpresent. Take a walk in a park, go hiking, or simply take a moment to smell flowers or sit outside and watch the birds. The sights, sounds, and smells of nature can help you feel more connected and reduce stress.
- **Deep Breathing:** Whenever you feel your mind wandering or stress creeping in, take a few minutes to practice deep breathing. Inhale deeply through your nose, hold for a few seconds, and then exhale slowly through your mouth. This simple exercise can help calm your mind and bring you back to the present.

Bpresent teaches us that life is too precious to be lived on the outside, on fast-forward. It encourages us to slow down, savor each moment, and make conscious choices that align with our values and goals. Fully engaging in the moment, loving deeply, laughing freely, and living intentionally. The power of Bpresent lies in its simplicity and accessibility any time we need it. It never requires a grand gesture or perfect conditions and it only asks for mindfulness and intention in our thoughts and actions. Whether it's a joyful gathering with loved ones, the mundane chore of washing dishes, or the overwhelming pressure of life's demands, Bpresent provides for us with a tool to navigate it all with grace and resilience.

As you move forward, carry the essence of Bpresent into every aspect of your life. Remember to:

- Love Fully.
- Laugh Freely.
- Live in the Moment.

When times are tough, and being present feels like a challenge, remember that Bpresent is there to support you through it all. Grounding exercises, mindful practices, and prioritizing self-care can help you ease the tension of even the hardest of days. Making the most of every moment, living with intention, and finding joy along the journey, let's commit to Bpresent each day and embrace them all with power, joy, and light. The cool thing that happens when you're able to Bpresent is that you're better able to connect with the essence of who you are. You're more able to Byou, which brings us to the final Powerword in this book.

RemindHer: Live in the moment, fully engaged with the here and now, and appreciate your life as it unfolds.

CHAPTER 15:

Byou

"Be yourself, everyone else is already taken."

~SORIBEL MARTINEZ

Rae

My trip to the RISE conference was like a reset for me. I was absolutely terrified of leaving my kids for even a few nights. I wasn't expecting to get what I had gotten out of the conference. Even though I went in with no expectations, it wound up being a pivotal moment. I had two small kids at home, I was newly pregnant (naturally!), and full of the anxiety that accompanies mothers who have fertility struggles.

I had to Bbrave, I had to Bfearless to make myself get in the car, on that plane, and I am so grateful to myself for taking that plunge. My main takeaway from the conference was taking ownership in your life. Only you get to choose how you feel and only you get to decide how everyday feels in your life, At that point in my life, all my dreams were on hold. My son was one, my daughter was two and a half, I was 4 months pregnant and I had given so much to my kids that I lost myself almost completely. Taking myself out of my comfort zone allowed me to find myself again and reignite my power within.

Because of this time away, I started thinking about me again, the real me, not mother me, or business owner me, jewelry designer me, or caretaker me. I had simply been going through the motions at work, and at home. I wasn't making choices about what my passions and hobbies were and what makes me feel like me. I had stopped everything that had to do with me, when in reality, falling back on my kids was just an easy way to not have to invest in myself. I had lost my pink, just like mama flamingos lose theirs, and like them, it was my job to find out how to feed myself so I could get my pink back. But, unlike the flamingo, I didn't get quite the same shade of pink back, it was a new pink, a new version of me. We're always changing, and meeting a new version of ourselves. My only request? Make sure you like who you're becoming.

When people ask who you are, do you respond with the roles you play? Teacher, doctor, lawyer, wife, mother, auntie… or do you list things you love to do? Hike, swim, travel, cook . . .

So many of us define ourselves in these roles, but I think that's problematic. Why? Because if you define yourself based on things you enjoy or roles you play, it limits your potential. You weren't created as a limited entity. You were created for constant expansion of your heart, mind, and soul. If you need proof of that, just talk to any mother with more than one child. Every woman I know had a moment while they were pregnant with their second baby when they wondered if they'd be able to love the new baby as much as they love their first. That first taste of motherhood filled them near to bursting and they can't imagine feeling that for another being.

Then the baby comes, and, even if not right away, the mother's heart expands before rapidly filling to capacity again. This is what our hearts and spirits are designed to do, expand, and then fill, repeatedly.

So, I fulfill a lot of roles, and I have some hobbies and friendships I hold dear, but none of that is who I am. None of that defines me.

Byou is about staying connected to the essence of who you are. Our hope for you is that as you incorporate these Powerwords, or your own Powerword into your life, that you find a way to Byou on the good days, the hard days, and every day in between.

How do you stay connected to who you are?

Remember your essence, and find the things that keep you most connected to yourself.

Chrissy

While vacationing with a family we've done business with for years, I was reminded of how the world can try to change who we are or mold us into what others think we must be. Arielle, the four-year-old daughter, played in the sand while her parents and I chatted. "Chrissy, she's so shy," said her mother. "We're trying to help her in school, reminding her she needs to speak up," said her father, concerned about their daughter.

Sensing a shared trait between us, I asked, "May I talk to her for a bit? I was quite shy as a child myself." With an encouraging nod, her mother sent Arielle over to me.

As she sat beside me on the sandy beach, Arielle held my hand without hesitation. Her beautiful brown curls fluttered in the breeze, and her giant blue eyes did not blink as they met mine. "Can I look into your eyes so I can count the magic sparkles?" I whispered, hoping to see her smile. Her lips fluttered in a quick smile, and she moved her gaze between me and the toys littering the sand.

"When I was a little girl, I was very shy too. It's okay when your mom and dad tell you to speak up; that's important. But remember, your shyness isn't just a challenge—it's also your superpower. It makes you an amazing listener. Can you remember that for me and never forget that you were born to be a listener?"

Her curls bounced as Arielle nodded. I smiled at her mother who said, "Thank you for that, Chrissy. You're right. It is good for her to be who she is."

I paused, reflecting on how this moment mirrored what I often forget about myself. When life is busy, and work is soaking up tons of energy, my kids' needs are overwhelming, and my husband gets called into work early or made to stay late, I often forget the essence of who I am. It's not like all of me disappears, but glimmers and pieces fade until I start to feel disconnected, adrift, and unsettled. That's why we created the Byou bracelet. It's a visual reminder that you are not your roles. You are not the things you do for others. You are not worthy because of what you accomplish. You are worthy because you are you.

In a conversation with our ghostwriter about this book, I realized I'd forgotten to have fun. I am fun and playful, but in the business of life, I forgot about that. So this week I decided to reignite the playful side of me. I wore my Byou bracelet and reminded myself to find some fun in every day.

The next week was interesting. I started by listening to a podcast by Glennon Doyle, author of Untamed about not knowing how to have fun. Yep, I started a journey to have fun with research. But, what I learned there is that I'm not alone and lots of women have the same experience. It's not that deep, we can just decide to find more fun.

I added the word music to my calendar to remind myself to turn on some tunes when my family and I are tackling chores. That evening, while I slogged through the dishes piled in the sink, Scarlet, Kash, and Danny started singing and dancing with me. Did it make me enjoy doing dishes? Nope, that part still stunk, but I was enjoying my people and my heart felt lighter.

Next I swapped my podcasts and self-development audible habit for music on my commute to work. It's twelve minutes, and while I obviously believe in self-development, I also believe in fun, and I decided to be better at balancing the two.

I took a walk on the same path I always use and this time I actually stopped to enjoy the smell of the lilac bush I pass every day and typically just float by.

Then I got caught in a storm. But since I decided to have fun again, it didn't deter me. Instead, I found fun in the storm. I went to coffee with a friend, Tammy. We meet once a month to laugh, cry, and fight over who pays for the coffee. I walked over from the jewelry store, she was already there, and then a thunderstorm started, and not one of those slow summer storms, this was an absolute downpour. I asked Tammy for a ride.

"I'll give you a ride, but the car is far away and you're all dressed for work. I'll get the car and pick you up at the front. I get to work from home so I don't care if I get drenched."

Something about that didn't feel right.

"I'll just go with you," I said, "I can just put my hair up and who cares about makeup." I didn't recognize myself as the words spilled out.

We stood under the awning of the coffee shop and it was like the storm decided to hit the next level. She got that look in her eye and took off running. I chased her. We stopped under awnings on our way to the car to catch our breath, but it didn't matter, we were drenched.

We made it to her car, my shoes filled with water, hair plastered to my head, and makeup completely gone. We had tears in our eyes from the laughter. She dropped me off and I walked into the jewelry store to a chorus of, "Oh my gosh! Chrissy, you have curly hair?"

That week was different, and each week since has been too because of the visual reminder to Byou on my wrist. I was looking for fun just because of the power of words to influence our behavior. Make no mistake, words hold power. They have the power to hurt you, leave you feeling empty, and steal your desire to live. But that means they also have the power to lift you up, reinvigorate you and remind you of who you are meant to B.

The next time you find yourself feeling off-kilter, ask yourself what parts of you that you haven't used lately.

Is your creative side starving because you're too focused on productivity?

Does your free spirit need a car ride with the windows down?

Does your spiritual side need a visit to church or a hike up a mountain to feel alive?

Or maybe you're like me and you forget to have fun.

Our hope, for you and for Arielle, is to remember who you were before the world told you who you should be. Reconnect with that essence. Find the things that keep you most connected to yourself. That's how you tap into your true power, on the good days, the bad days, and every day in between.

As we finish the last chapter of this book, this labor of love that we cannot wait to give you, we will share a story about our visit with a friend who just had a baby. During that visit, we were blessed with the opportunity to look into that new being's eyes and enjoy the sparkle of new life, of the essence of what makes us human. Now, do us a favor, go look in the mirror. Do your eyes sparkle with delight, or mischief, or joy? When was the last time you looked in your own eyes and saw the sparkle? You are as miraculous now as you were as a baby, as magical as when you were a little girl. We all are. We grow up and take on roles that sometimes make us forget our magic. Byou is about remembering that magic.

RemindHer: Stay true to yourself and honor the person you are becoming.

CONCLUSION

Chrissy

Dear Reader,

As we come to the close of our journey together in "Ignite YOUR Power Within," I want you to remember one thing: the power to thrive lies within you, not just on the good days, but especially on the hard ones, and indeed, every day in between.

Visual reminders are our secret tools—simple, yet profound cues that anchor us back to who we are and who we aspire to B.

Within the cozy confines of my home, each room holds reminders that both ground and uplift my family and me . In my kitchen, where family meals blend flavors and laughter, a softly glowing candle is a symbol to sit down, have family dinner, and be truly present with those I love.

Moving into the living room, a space designed for relaxation and rejuvenation, a serene yoga symbol rests on the coffee table . It is meant to remind anyone who enters to shed the chaos of the outside world and breathe in tranquility.

In the area where I dress each morning, my jewelry collection including Powerword bracelets hold a special place. Each piece I wear has meaning—Grandma Dolly's bracelet we share, the rings symbolizing our love story, the earrings that remind me to Shine

Bright, the diamond necklace that means endless belief in me. Then each Powerword bracelet carries a word, a mantra, that fuels me with strength for the day ahead. Slipping a bracelet over my wrist is as much a part of my morning routine as my first cup of coffee—it's a ritual that adorns my spirit as well as my body.

Our bedroom wall at the foot of our bed houses a collage of art . This isn't just any decoration—it's a collection of photos from a couple's shoot with my husband, interspersed with images and words that reflect the pillars of our relationship. Love, partnership, mutual support, and laughter are all captured here, reminding us of our journey together and the dreams we continue to build.

Perched on my windowsill, a small statue of a cardinal watches over the room. Cardinals are one of the signs I look for to know I'm moving in the right direction. It reminds me that I am never alone, that spirit guides are always near, whispering courage and offering guidance when I need it most.

My son Kash has framed words of encouragement on his bedroom walls made from the two pieces of wood he broke with his bare hands at Tae Kwon Do. I want my children to grow up knowing that visual reminders and the words they speak to themselves are powerful. Those words remind him he can do anything and to believe in himself no matter what he faces.

And then there are the affirmation coffee mugs in the kitchen—each one chosen to match the 'vibe' I need for the day. Whether it's "choose happy" "get after it" or "see the good," these mugs do more than hold coffee; they hold intentions for the day.

These RemindHers are part of my mind, body and spirit-care practice so that I can show up every day as the most powerful version of myself. In the pages of this book I've shared stories of how Powerwords influence my life, and you've heard from other women who've embraced this practice as well. Now, I want to invite you to incorporate The Power to B into your daily life.

Find ways to remind yourself when you need to Bfearless and try something different, or when you need to channel Bfierce to push through obstacles. Let Blimitless help you chase your dreams, and stay open to signs you're on the right path. Keep yourself healthy in the ways you're able, and Bstrong when challenges throw you off course. Maintain your own personal sexiness, and know that Bsexy is about more than how much time you spend between the sheets. Bbrave when you find yourself facing uncertainty because uncertainty is a guarantee in this beautiful, messy life. Find your people so you can Bsupported in all you do, and remember to Bkind to yourself as well as others. Bbada** whenever you need a little sass to get you through the day and greet each morning with a grateful heart so you can Bblessed. Bpresent in each moment in your life—soak up the joy, and feel the sadness that will inevitably come—feeling those emotions is what creates a full, rich life. And, above all else, remember to Byou on the hard days, the good days, and all the days in between because when you live in alignment with your values and goals anything is possible and your dreams become probable.

The point I want to drive home, though, is learning and growing in your spirit through reading, and searching for new ways to harness your power and create more joy will only improve your life if you take action. So now, I want you to take a tiny action step. What reminders will you place in your space and on your body so you never forget the joy and strength you possess? Perhaps it's a Powerword bracelet that whispers courage at the start of your day, or a candle in your kitchen that invites you to breathe deeply and cherish the moment with your family. Make a decision, and then take action and place that RemindHer.

Embrace these RemindHers with love and intention. Let them be your companions as you navigate the challenges and beauties of life. Place them where they can uplift your spirit and ignite your joy—the handwritten message on your mirror, the note from your loved one, or even a tattoo that marks your skin with the symbols of your inner strength.

And as you weave these RemindHers into your daily life, use the visual reminder of simply seeing this book by your bedside or in your tote to remind you, too, the magic of the words we've shared. Pick it back up from time to time for a refresh and flip to that Powerword chapter you feel will guide you in any moment you may need. Just as I believed as a child in the power of magic words to summon rainbows or unicorns, believe in the power of your actions and words to transform your world. Each day is a canvas, and you hold the brush. Paint it with vigor, kindness, and a touch of whimsy.

So, my dear reader, as we part ways in this book, know that you are not alone. You are part of a vibrant community of women, each striving, each supporting one another. Please, join us on social media, and dive into https://www.thepowertob.com so we can stay connected. Together, let's find joy in the hard days, relish the good ones, and cherish every moment in between. You are ready. You have everything you need within yourself—and as you set your reminders I will B there cheering you on, always.

XXOO, Chrissy

Rae

Life is fleeting, and the reality is that we aren't guaranteed tomorrow, let alone five years from now. So, what are you waiting for? The time to find your purpose and live it is now. If you're uncertain about where to begin, start small—focus on gratitude. Gratitude has the power to transform your life; it ignites a brightness that can lead you to greater things.

There was a time when I was a new mom, overwhelmed by the mental and physical challenges that role brought. I found myself scrolling through social media, absorbing the banter about motherhood. Although it gave me a good laugh now and again, it was in those moments that I realized how unfulfilling that was for me. Social media can be a positive space, but only if you're filling your feed with messages that uplift and inspire you to live a better, more engaged connected life.

Starting with gratitude can change everything. It's an intoxicating practice that will spiral you into a place where you're constantly seeking to do more, live better, and be more present in the world around you.

If you're someone who feels stuck, unsure of where to start, know that you're not alone. It's easy to feel burdened by the past or anxious about the future. But remember, anything you hold onto from the past is only holding you back from moving forward. Stay where your feet are—be present in this moment, without looking too far ahead or dwelling on what's behind.

As we part, I invite you to join our community, where you can continue this journey with support and inspiration. We're offering a special discount on a piece of Power to B jewelry as a token of our appreciation. If you visit https://www.thepowertob.com/ and use the code PTB10 you'll get 10 percent off any piece of jewelry. Wear it as a reminder of your strength, your purpose, and your commitment to living your best life.

Remember, living a consistently high-vibration life takes work. Our brains aren't naturally wired for it, but with intention and practice, you can cultivate the resilience needed to face the challenges of our rapidly changing world. As women, we are the energy source in our homes, and our positive impact ripples through to everyone around us.

To my mom readers, your children may not always listen to what you say, but they are always watching what you do. Set an example for them—show them what it means to take care of their minds, bodies, and spirits so they don't give too much of themselves. If you're caught in a cycle of busyness and exhaustion, remember, you're the only one who can break free. Say no when you need to, and don't be afraid to prioritize your well-being.

The life you want is within your reach. The power to live it fully lies within you. So go on—find your purpose, make your mark, and live your dreams. The time to start is now.

XXOO, Rae

We'd love to invite you to visit our website at https://www.thepowertob.com/resources/ where we have free resources intended to deepen your Powerword practice and help you find more joy on the good days, the hard days, and every day in between.

SCAN ME

THE POWER TO B COMMUNITY STORIES

These courageous people have chosen to share their stories with you because stories connect us and through connection, we find strength. Our hope is that you see yourself in at least one of these stories, and use what these women share as a RemindHer that you have The Power to B within you.

Soribel Martinez, a Dominican immigrant and single mom who started a massively successful group mental health practice and now coaches other therapists in doing the same. You can learn more about her and her books at www.soribelmartinez.com.

Karen Mooad, a fourteen-year colon cancer survivor, mother to seven children and foster children, and dedicated nonprofit volunteer wears Bstrong.

Dr. Deb Feldman, director of Maternal Fetal Medicine for Hartford Healthcare, who specializes in caring for high-risk pregnant patients with both expertise and empathy. Deb battled breast cancer while continuing to care for her patients, and she is still out there winning 5Ks and competing in triathlons.

Beverly Canepari and Lora Karam, best friends and creators of the Unlocking Connecticut website, are dedicated to discovering and sharing Connecticut's hidden treasures. They committed to creating a business together that improves the lives of residents across their state.

Judy Flynn, a woman who's overcome many obstacles including divorce and single parenthood to create a successful smoothie chain called The Fresh Monkee.

Sara Horwitz, who overcame health issues and launched her business to educate children about reptiles, especially snakes, and inspire young women to pursue careers in science. She recently appeared on the Kelly Clarkson Show and is inspiring the next generation women scientists.

Kara Welz says she loves the power word *Bstrong* because it reminds her of her fight against cancer. She never takes her bracelet off.

Tiffany Ryan says the power word, *Bstrong*, resonates with her the most because it reminds her that there's nothing in her life that she can't handle. Since she has one of the original bracelets, she welded it on as she never took it off.

Kristilee LaHaye says her power word is Bbada** and that it reminds her of Chrissy when the idea of The Power to B was just a concept. After attending a women's conference in 2020, she realized that she is fortunate enough to have witnessed a powerful woman bringing an idea to life. When in need of a little encouragement, she rubs the onyx stone for some extra Bbada** energy.

Jen Staskiewicz says that her bracelet depicting the power word, *BFearless*, is a reminder that she can face and overcome adversity while giving herself grace.

Sandy Cassanelli says that the power word, *Bstrong*, is her favorite because it reminds her of her courage during her battle with cancer.

Tammy Ferris says her power word, *Byou*, is her reminder that she is enough and is loved. As an entrepreneur, there's lots of uncertainty in her work but the bracelet serves as a little nudge of encouragement in the moments when she needs it. When she needs said encouragement, she gently squeezes the stone with her thumb and index finger like a mini-hug.

Nichole Baribault says her power word, *Bfearless,* reminds her of the quote, "Sometimes life takes you in a direction you never saw yourself going, but it turns out to be the best road you have ever taken."

Jodi Lussier says that her bracelets have the Powerword 'BStrong' and 'Bfierce' on them. 'Bstrong' is in honor of her sister who lost her battle with cancer and her friend who's been fighting cancer for a decade while "Bfierce" is a reminder that she got through a difficult time in her life and will be able to do it again. She always touches the onyx for strength, positivity and gratitude.

Bethany says that the power word, *Bstrong,* is her way of reminding herself that she can do anything no matter how hard it may be. She rarely takes her bracelet off but when she does, she makes sure to have "Bstrong" facing toward her.

Sara Moore says the power word *Blimitless* is her reminder to persevere through her own insecurities and fears while acknowledging that they are the roadblock to success and happiness in her life.

Stephen Alexander says the word *Bgrateful* reminds him of his family. He never takes it off because whenever he looks down, it fills him with gratitude.

Caitlin Glynn says the word *Bstrong* is her reminder to be strong throughout everything she experiences. At 11:11 a.m., Caitlin makes a conscious effort to think about the word and how she can use it to charge her mindset for the moment.

Susan Karp says the bracelet with the power word *Bstrong* is a way to remember the challenges she faced and hopes that her strength will encourage others. Looking at her bracelet is her reminder to purposely start each day with a positive attitude.

Cherie says the power word *Bstrong* is her physical reminder to be strong in times when she feels overwhelmed or defeated. She puts her bracelet on while getting ready at the start of each day so that she has the constant reminder to be strong during the inevitable moments where she feels overwhelmed.

Annette Hainey says her bracelet with the word *Bbada*** is a testament to her strength and independence. She has worn different power words depending on how she felt and what she needed for herself.

Bridget Camara wears a bracelet with the power word *Bfearless* as a reminder to keep going in moments of adversity.

Kristi Sharkevich dons a bracelet with the power word *Blimitless* as a reminder that she is capable of pursuing her passions and overcoming struggles while reinforcing that her potential knows no bounds. She has it soldered on as a permanent reminder.

Chrissy Monaco Dimauro owns a bracelet with the power word *Bfierce* on it. It serves as a reminder that she's been lucky enough to be in her friend's lives. Every morning while she's getting dressed she'll put it on last and head out the door.

Jackie J has a bracelet toting the word *Bstrong* as a reminder of her favorite quote: "What the caterpillar calls the end of the world, the world calls butterfly."

Alisa Picerno says her favorite power word is *Bpresent* because it reminds her to "keep her head where my feet are," meaning to slow down and appreciate the simple things in life. She likes to run her fingers over the word and reflect on how she's going to achieve it that day.

Jennifer Ganley says the power word *Bstrong* is her favorite because it reminds her to not let the hard days win. Every day when she wakes up and puts it on, she thinks back to the day before and all the ways I was strong, then commits to being strong again.

Liz Cavanna says her bracelet with the word *Bfearless* is her favorite because it reminds her of all the difficult obstacles and how there is only one way through them. She will glance down and rub her fingers over the letters to provide regulation when negative thoughts become overwhelming.

Erin O'Grady says her bracelet that says *Bbada*** is her personal favorite because it reminds her that her family has her back and believes in her as she rebuilds her life after a divorce and career change.

Lisa DiBenedetto says her favorite power word is *Bgrateful* because it reminds her to look around and realize that she's still here.

Stephanie Tishler shared, "Each bracelet I own has its own story. It began with BStrong when I was in the throes of supporting several friends fighting their way through breast cancer battles. We all wore the BStrong reminder together so that we knew no one was alone. Next came Bbrave, which was my word during the early days of the pandemic. Like nothing we had ever dealt with before, it was a scary time in our lives, and all I wanted to do was hide from the world, but I couldn't. As a mom, a wife, and a coach, too many people relied on me for support, confidence, and encouragement. But I couldn't offer that if I didn't have it myself. I dug deep and turned to the things I knew would make me feel brave—running, writing and staying focused on caring for those I loved. The Bbrave bracelet was a gift from Chrissy after a tearful run. It was a pivotal moment during those early days of COVID-19. My most recent bracelet purchase was Bbada** because, well, I am one, even if I didn't realize I was! It was an honor to be one of the first interviewed by Christine and Salt on their radio show for their Bada** Woman of The Week feature. They talked about the impact I've had on my clients, daughters, and friends. I do this by setting a high bar with the expectation that I will provide support throughout. I relentlessly believe in people and connect them to others and resources to make their goals happen. When I am attached to a specific word, I don't take it off! I look at it throughout the day because "What we focus on, we become, right?"

ABOUT THE AUTHORS

Chrissy and Raeann started The Power to B brand when they both struggled with infertility and needed daily reminders of their ability to handle the hard parts of life. Firm believers in the power within each of us and the signs that guide our lives, Chrissy and Raeann aim to reconnect readers with their joy and purpose. Through this book, they offer a blend of fun, playfulness, and seriousness, sharing how a Powerword practice has helped them navigate life's challenges while enjoying the journey by helping readers start this Powerword practice or inspire them to find a version of their own.

Chrissy has always believed in the magic of words. As a child, she would sit in the back of her parents' beige station wagon, imagining that creating the perfect unique word could conjure rainbows and unicorns. This belief in the power of words inspired sisters, Chrissy and Raeann to create a jewelry collection of elevated powerword bracelets called The Power to B Collection.

Chrissy is a mother of two children, jewelry designer, gem-ologist, certified health coach, wife, daughter, and sister. Beyond these roles, she is a loving, passionate, and determined individual who is creative, adventurous, and sometimes an overthinker wrestling with self-doubt. She is spiritual, energetic, grateful, silly, and knows when to get down to business. Chrissy hates doing dishes but loves connecting with people.

Raeann is a highly creative entrepreneur, mother of three children, and a woman with a dream of shattering the gender roles typically assigned to women. Rae is a positive thinker with a touch of OCD. She finds peace near the water and believes anything with bubbles makes life more fun.

Raeann proves that women can have it all and do whatever fuels their mind, body, and soul. She rejects traditional gender roles in homes, businesses, and society, encouraging others to march to the beat of their own drum.

A free ebook edition is available with the purchase of this book.

To claim your free ebook edition:

1. Visit MorganJamesBOGO.com
2. Sign your name CLEARLY in the space
3. Complete the form and submit a photo of the entire copyright page
4. You or your friend can download the ebook to your preferred device

Morgan James
BOGO™

A **FREE** ebook edition is available for you or a friend with the purchase of this print book.

CLEARLY SIGN YOUR NAME ABOVE

Instructions to claim your free ebook edition:
1. Visit MorganJamesBOGO.com
2. Sign your name CLEARLY in the space above
3. Complete the form and submit a photo of this entire page
4. You or your friend can download the ebook to your preferred device

Print & Digital Together Forever.

Snap a photo

Free ebook

Read anywhere